NORTH CAROLINA
STATE BOARD OF COMMUNITY COLLEGES
LIBRARIES
WAKE TECHNICAL COMMUNITY COLLEGE

Y0-CUN-869

WITHDRAWN

Southern Literary Studies
Louis D. Rubin, Jr., Editor

Selected Essays
1965–1985

Thomas Daniel Young

Louisiana State University Press   *Baton Rouge and London*

Copyright © 1990 by Louisiana State University Press
All rights reserved
Manufactured in the United States of America
First printing

99 98 97 96 95 94 93 92 91 90   5 4 3 2 1

Designer: Amanda McDonald Key
Typeface: Baskerville
Typesetter: G&S Typesetters, Inc.
Printer and binder: Thomson-Shore, Inc.

LIBRARY OF CONGRESS
CATALOGING-IN-PUBLICATION DATA

Young, Thomas Daniel, 1919–
  [Essays. Selections]
  Selected essays, 1965–1985 / Thomas Daniel Young.
   p. cm. — (Southern literary studies)
  ISBN 0-8071-1559-2 (alk. paper)
  1. American literature—Southern States—History and criticism.
  2. Ransom, John Crowe, 1888–1974—Criticism and interpretation.
  3. Southern States in literature.   I. Title.   II. Series.
PS261.Y62   1990
810.9′975—dc20   89-13692
                                                        CIP

The paper in this book meets the guidelines for permanence
and durability of the Committee on Production Guidelines for Book
Longevity of the Council on Library Resources. ∞

Contents

Narration as Creative Act: The Role of Quentin Compson in Absalom, Absalom!	1
Ransom's Critical Theories: Image and Idea	19
Ransom's Critical Theories: Structure and Texture	34
A Little Divergence: The Critical Theories of John Crowe Ransom and Cleanth Brooks	50
John Crowe Ransom: A Major Minor Poet	73
Our Two Worthies: Robert Frost and John Crowe Ransom	84
The Little Houses Against the Great	94
The Evolution of "Lee in the Mountains"	107
Brother to Dragons: *A Meditation on the Basic Nature of Man*	142
"The Lady Ageth but Is Not Stoop'd": Agrarianism in Contemporary Southern Fiction	153
Index	175

Selected Essays, 1965–1985

Narration as Creative Act: The Role of Quentin Compson in Absalom, Absalom!

MANY commentators have pointed out that Faulkner devoted a great deal of time—to some even a disproportionate amount—to the Judith-Henry-Charles love triangle in a story that is ostensibly about the rise and fall of Thomas Sutpen. Despite the fact, too, that Faulkner exerts considerable artistic energy in pointing out that Shreve McCannon and Quentin are both unreliable narrators, their version is usually considered the reliable one—not only of what Thomas Sutpen and his family did (and even the actions of some persons who might not have belonged to the family) but *why* they did what they did. The credibility of Shreve and Quentin to most readers is not diminished by Quentin's deep emotional involvement in the tale he is telling or by Shreve's insatiable desire to make every detail of the story he creates (with Quentin's urging) fit neatly into a preconceived pattern. This desire for artistic unity is so great that Shreve ignores any facts that he considers unnecessary to his sense of structure, and, as Brooks and others have pointed out, he creates new ones as he thinks they are needed. Even Faulkner's insistence that "nobody saw the truth intact"[1] has not affected the view of many critics. They still insist that the conclusions drawn by Quentin and Shreve are more nearly correct than are those of the other narrators. Faulkner even indicates, in a letter to Malcolm Cowley, that it is Quentin's story, not his, that Quen-

---

This essay originally appeared, in slightly different form, in *Faulkner, Modernism and Film: Faulkner and Yoknapatawpha, 1978*, ed. Evans Harrington and Ann J. Abadie (Jackson, Miss., 1979). Reprinted by permission of the University Press of Mississippi.

1. Frederick L. Gwynn and Joseph L. Blotner (eds.), *Faulkner in the University: Class Conferences at the University of Virginia, 1957–1958* (New York, 1985), 273.

tin is responsible for whatever symbolic overtones the story may contain. Another statement by Faulkner, however, has not been ignored. When the reader has read all the different versions of what happened in *Absalom, Absalom!*, Faulkner says, he should offer his own view. With this encouragement, perhaps, this work of art, one of the most evocative and imaginatively designed novels ever written in America, has also become one of the most written about. Faulkner even goes on to say that the reader's view—"this fourteenth image" of the blackbird—might be the "truth."

The reading I offer of this much interpreted novel—feeling a little like Fra Lippo Lippi from Browning's poem as I do so—is based on the following hypotheses: 1) that the Quentin Compson who appears as character and narrator in *Absalom, Absalom!* is the same youth who had the disturbing and destroying experiences related in *The Sound and the Fury*, and 2) that the narrative he creates in *Absalom, Absalom!* is vastly influenced by the impact these experiences had on him. Given the opportunity and the motivation of Mr. Compson's letter announcing Rosa Coldfield's death, he and Shreve attempt to supply missing details of the Sutpen legend and to furnish plausible motivations for some of the improbable actions of the participants in that story. Quentin is the principal agent, therefore, in the creation of a story that gives temporary relief to the powerful emotional disturbances that will ultimately destroy him. The story Quentin creates assuages momentarily the deep feelings of frustration and despair produced by his unmanly and ineffectual behavior before Dalton Ames, a seducer of Quentin's sister, Caddy. The story he and Shreve piece together out of the few facts Quentin has learned from his father and Rosa Coldfield helps Quentin to accept momentarily the incestuous love he suspects he feels for Caddy. As narrator of much of the action of *Absalom, Absalom!*, Quentin creates a story in which he can participate vicariously as both brother-seducer and brother-avenger.

In August, 1909, Quentin Compson discovers that his sister, Caddy, is having an affair with Dalton Ames, a young construction worker who has recently moved with his company into Jefferson. (It was not the first time Quentin had known or suspected that Caddy was giving herself to men, and each incident as it occurred had left Quentin more confused, less certain of exactly how he felt toward Caddy.) His confusion is confounded by the fact that he can neither control her behavior nor punish those who participate with Caddy in her improper acts. Once, he throws coal at the pimply faced boy who is necking with Caddy among the trees outside their front door. On another afternoon, Caddy comes home, and as soon as Benjy, her younger, idiot brother, sees her (or smells her), he begins "pulling at her dress," and they go in the house, with him yelling at her and pushing her up the stairs to the bathroom door. There he stops her and backs her against the door, "yelling and trying to shove her into the bathroom."[2] By making her scrub with soap, Benjy is trying to remove from her the scent she has applied to attract the boys. Quentin says later that Benjy can smell death, that he knew, by how Caddy smelled, exactly when Caddy committed her first sex act. On that evening, soap will not remove the scent, and when Caddy comes into the kitchen where T. P. is feeding Benjy, Benjy begins to howl. Caddy rushes out of the house; Quentin follows her down to the branch where she lies with "her head on the sand spit the water flowing about her hips there was a little more light in the water her shirt half saturated flopped along her flanks" (*SF*, 186). When Caddy sees Quentin standing on the bank, she asks if Benjy is still crying. Quentin says he is and tells her to get out of the water, but she does not move. He tells her again and she comes out on the bank, and he asks her if she loves the man to whom she has given herself. She takes his hand and puts it on her breast, under which he can feel her heart thudding. She answers "no," and he asks if *he* made her do it, but before she can answer, Quentin promises to kill the boy before Mr. Compson can find out about it. Then, he says, they will take the money with which he is supposed to pay his Harvard tuition and run away together. Still lying on her back, she places his hand on her throat and says "Poor Quentin . . . youve never done that have you" (*SF*, 188–89). She lies there with his head against her chest, and he asks if she remembers the day she muddied her drawers in the branch when their grandmother died. (This crucial scene will be examined in some detail later.) She tells him good night and asks him to meet her later at the

---

2. William Faulkner, *The Sound and the Fury* (New York, 1954), 85. Hereinafter cited by page number in the text.

branch, saying now she must meet someone. He sees her and some man with their heads close together. She tells Quentin to go on home, but he says he is going to take a walk. He goes close enough to town to see the courthouse clock and circles back by the Compson house and notes as he passes that the light is out in Benjy's room. He goes back to the branch and lies on the bank with his face close to the ground so he cannot smell the honeysuckle. After a while, Caddy comes back from her date and offers herself to him twice. He tells her to shut up and asks her, "Do you love him now." She can only answer, "I dont know," and urges him not to cry because, she says, "Im bad . . . [and] you cant help it" (*SF*, 195–96).

But Quentin has found out what he wants to know. No longer is the source of his distress a nameless, faceless quality that he knows only as man. He is a distinct, separate, human creature, an individualized man named Dalton Ames. For two or three days Quentin seeks out Dalton before seeing him going into the barbershop, where he confronts him. But Dalton says they can't talk there and promises to meet Quentin at one o'clock on the bridge outside of town. When they meet at the barbershop, Dalton's only concern seems to be for Caddy, asking two or three times: "she all right . . . she need me for anything" (*SF*, 197). Quentin does not respond but assures him he will meet him at the bridge at one o'clock.

As one would expect from a brother who loves his sister, Quentin is determined to defend her honor in the respected tradition of the culture to which he belongs. He tells T. P. to saddle Prince and have him at the side door, but when Caddy keeps asking him where he is going, he decides to walk. He leaves the house, walking slowly down the drive, but he begins to run as soon as he thinks he is out of sight. As he approaches the bridge, he sees Dalton leaning on the rail with a piece of bark in his hand, from which he is breaking pieces and dropping them into the water. Quentin comes up to him and says, "I came to tell you to leave town" (*SF*, 198). Dalton doesn't seem to hear him and continues to drop the pieces of bark into the water and watch them float downstream. Quentin repeats his ultimatum and Dalton asks quietly, "Did she send you to me." Quentin responds that nobody sent him, not her, not even his father; "Ill give you until sundown to leave town." Dalton lays the bark on the railing and with three swift motions, rolls a cigarette, lights it, and flicks the match over the rail. Again he speaks quietly: "What . . . if I dont leave" (*SF*, 198).

"Ill kill you," Quentin responds; "dont think . . . just because I look like a kid to you" (*SF*, 198). Quentin's hands begin to shake on the rail and he is afraid to try to hide them for fear Dalton will see how excited he is. Then Dalton asks him his name, saying, "Benjys the natural isn't he." Again Quentin says, "Ill give you till sundown." Then Dalton asks him not to take it so hard, that if it had not been him it would have been someone else. To Quentin's question "Did you ever have a sister did you," Dalton responds, "No but theyre all bitches." Quentin can no longer control himself and strikes out at Dalton: "I hit him my open hand beat the impulse to shut it to his face his hand moved as fast as mine the cigarette went over the rail I swung with the other hand he caught it too before the cigarette reached the water he held both my wrists in the same hand his other hand flicked to his armpit under his coat behind him the sun slanted and a bird singing somewhere beyond the sun we looked at one another while the bird singing he turned my hand loose" (*SF*, 199). Taking the bark from the rail, Dalton tosses it into the water and lets it float almost out of sight. Without aiming the pistol he hits the large piece of bark and then two smaller ones, no larger than a silver dollar. He hands the pistol to Quentin, saying, "Youll need it from what you said Im giving you this one because youve seen what it do." Again, Quentin remembers, "I hit him I was still trying to hit him long after he was holding my wrists but I still tried then it was like I was looking at him through a piece of coloured glass I could hear my blood and then I could see the sky again and branches against it and the sun slanting through them and he holding me on my feet." Quentin doesn't realize immediately what is happening to him— he does not know he has fainted—so he asks Dalton if he had hit him. Dalton lies and answers, "Yes how do you feel." Then he offers Quentin his horse to get back home on. Dalton leaves, and Quentin, utterly crushed, leans against a tree, his mind completely filled with one emasculating thought: "I . . . just passed out like a girl." When Caddy comes up, having heard the shots and thinking Dalton might have killed Quentin, she says she has told Dalton never to speak to her again. Quentin asks her if she loves him; she takes his hand and puts it against her throat, and when he says, at her request, "Dalton Ames," he feels the blood surging "in strong accelerating beats" (*SF*, 200–203).

Soon after this confrontation with Dalton Ames, Quentin tells his father that he has committed incest with Caddy. But Mr. Compson knows his son, or thinks he does, and recognizes Quentin's terrible confession for the lie it is. He tells Quentin he should not be upset over his sister's promiscuity, that only a man would put much value on a woman's chastity. What Quentin should do, he remembers Mr. Compson's saying, is to leave early and take a month's vacation in Maine before the fall term at Harvard begins. We know, however, that Quentin does not take his father's advice; instead, he spends September, 1909, in Jefferson, because there on one afternoon and evening he hears from his father and Miss Rosa Coldfield, the old maid daughter of a deceased local merchant, the details of the most fascinating and bewildering tale that legend-rich Jefferson can boast of. Like all the other residents of the town, Quentin is aware of the legend of Thomas Sutpen and his family, but in these conversations in September, 1909, with Rosa Coldfield, Sutpen's sister-in-law, and Mr. Compson, whose father was Sutpen's best friend in Jefferson, Quentin must have had his memory jogged; surely he learned some new details.

Miss Coldfield tells Quentin her view of the Sutpen legend because she thinks he might become a literary man and reveal the facts of this tragic story to the world. What she doesn't know is that four months later in a dormitory room at Harvard, Quentin and his roommate will "create" a harrowing tale of revenge, incest, miscegenation, and fratricide out of the few details he garners from Rosa and Mr. Compson. She has concluded, she insists to Quentin that hot summer afternoon, that someone besides Clytie and the idiot Jim Bond, the grandson of Judith Sutpen's fiancé, Charles Bon, might be out at the ruins of Sutpen's Hundred, and she wants Quentin to go with her to investigate. The truth is that Miss Rosa has little to tell Quentin that is not already common knowledge around town. Thomas Sutpen came out of nowhere, without warning, brought with him a band of strange Negroes, and built the largest plantation in the county on land he had acquired from some Indians. When the plantation was barely completed he married Ellen Coldfield,

Rosa's older sister, upon whom he begat a son and a daughter. When Judith became engaged to Charles Bon, a law student from the university, Sutpen for no apparent reason forbade the marriage. Then the war came and Thomas, his son Henry, and Charles Bon went off to serve in the Confederate army.

Rosa can never understand, she tells Quentin, why her father allowed Ellen to marry Sutpen, who to her is an ogre; and his children, her niece and nephew, are far from normal. Just before Ellen dies, soon after the war began, Rosa promises her that she will care for her niece, though the niece is four years her senior. A year later, at her father's death, she moves out to the Sutpen place. After the war when Sutpen returns to the ruined plantation—the son Henry has already killed his sister's fiancé at the front gate—Rosa agrees to marry him but leaves abruptly one evening after he has made an unspeakable proposition to her. She returns to her little house in Jefferson, dons black, and lives the next forty-three years on the charity of her neighbors.

It is extremely doubtful, as I have said, that Quentin learns any new facts from Miss Rosa's version of the Sutpens. Most of the details of the legend that she knows—though she is the only narrator in the novel who had a personal acquaintance with Sutpen—must have been common knowledge around Jefferson. But Quentin must have been impressed with the highly subjective nature of Miss Rosa's account. She takes a few simple facts and creates a legend that gives some solace to the devastating wound she feels. Her only possible explanation for the insult Sutpen had given her—he says let's mate and if the issue is male, "I'll marry you"—is that he was a demon, a monster, a devil that rose out of the ground. She shapes the facts to make them meet her own emotional needs, a device Quentin will use later in his own behalf.

Later the same evening, while Quentin is waiting until it is time for him and Miss Rosa to go out to the old Sutpen place, Quentin hears other facts about Sutpen, some that Mr. Compson had learned from his father. Most of these facts are also well known and need not be rehearsed in detail here. Because he had been turned away from the front door of a Virginia plantation when he was thirteen or fourteen, Sutpen formulated a design. This "design" required that he have his own plantation, complete with manor house, servants, slaves, family, and respectability. First he went to the West Indies, where because of an act of personal valor and a long period of recuperation he came to know and was allowed to marry the daughter of the owner of the sugar plantation he was managing. When their first child was born, it became apparent to Sutpen (for some reason never fully explained in the novel) that this woman, through no fault of her own, could never fit into his "design." Consequently he divorced her, giving her far more than a fair share of their common property, and left. Then in June, 1833, he showed up in Jefferson, remained a few days, and disappeared, to return a short time later with a wagon filled with wild Negroes (two of whom were female) and a French architect. Out on the ten square miles he had acquired from Ikkemotubbe, Sutpen, his Negroes, and the French architect set about building the largest house in the county. After the house was built, though it had no windows, doors, or furniture, Sutpen began to invite citizens of the town to come out to drink and hunt or to watch the fights he had arranged between the Negroes or between himself and one of the Negroes. Finally, after the house had stood in its unfinished state for three years, Sutpen appeared in Jefferson again, this time with four wagons filled with mahogany, crystal, rugs, and chandeliers. Again, nobody was ever to know where the goods had come from. Immediately after the house was completed, he acquired the last piece of property he needed to be a respectable planter. He married the daughter of a poor but honest and devout small merchant of the town. Then, almost as if he were following his preconceived notion of the perfect plan, Sutpen had the son, to inherit and carry along the family name, and the daughter, to grace his household, to help her mother entertain, and in due time to allow him to enjoy the love and companionship of grandchildren.

His would seem the ideal family, and one which was the result of his own tenacious desire to mold his personal affairs exactly as he would have them be. In 1857, Henry, the son, enrolled at the University of Mississippi, and his second Christmas there he brought a friend, Charles Bon, home to spend the holidays. Bon was a sophisticated young man from New Orleans, several years older than Henry, and a man of mystery, worldly, elegant, apparently wealthy, with an ease of manners and a swaggering gallant air completely out of keeping with the atmosphere of a small provincial university less than ten years old. (Mr. Compson wondered how Bon got there in the first place.) When Henry brought Bon home again for a few days at the beginning of the summer of 1859, any casual observer could see that he was attempting to model himself after Charles in every respect, and immediately after the two boys left, Ellen Sutpen announced her daughter's engagement to Charles. Soon after Charles departed for New Orleans, Thomas Sutpen followed him.

The next Christmas, Henry brought Charles home with him again, but this time Henry and his father had a quarrel and both boys rode away. Soon thereafter war was declared, Thomas Sutpen became second in command of the regiment Colonel Sartoris raised in Jefferson, and Henry and Charles joined a company formed at the university.

Mr. Compson speculates on what Henry found, when he accompanied Charles to New Orleans, that disturbed him so deeply. "It would not . . . [have been] the mistress," Mr. Compson says, "or even the child, not even the negro mistress and even less the child because . . . Henry and Judith had grown up with a negro half sister of their own. . . . No: it would be the ceremony, a ceremony entered into, to be sure, with a negro, yet still a ceremony."[3] Mr. Compson thinks that Henry waited for Bon to denounce the woman and dissolve the marriage, that Henry objected not to bigamy but to the fact that Bon was making Judith a part of a harem.

As Mr. Compson recalls the facts of the war experience, Bon was commissioned shortly after the war began, but Henry remained a private. At Pittsburg Landing, Charles was wounded and Henry carried him back to safety. For four years, Mr. Compson insists, Henry gave Charles the opportunity to renounce the New Orleans mistress and child or, as Mr. Compson expresses Charles' thoughts, "For four years now I have given chance the opportunity to renounce for me, but it seems that I am doomed to live, that she and I are both doomed to live" (*AA*, 132). Both Henry and Charles thought that one or both of them would be killed, Mr. Compson says, thus making unnecessary a decision from either (Bon's is, will he marry a woman whom he thinks to

---

[3]. William Faulkner, *Absalom, Absalom!* (New York, 1965), 127. Hereinafter cited by page number in the text.

be his half-sister, and Henry's is, will he kill his own brother to keep the marriage from occurring?). When the war ended, both men were still alive, and the decision was still not made. As Mr. Compson describes the two men riding up to the gate of the Sutpen house, it seems to Quentin that he can almost see them, "facing one another at the gate. Inside the gate what was once a park now spread, unkempt, in shaggy desolation, with an air dreamy, remote and aghast . . . up to a huge house where a young girl waited in a wedding dress made from stolen scraps. . . . They faced one another on the two gaunt horses, two men, young, not yet in the world . . . with unkempt hair and faces gaunt and weathered." Quentin imagines Henry saying: "Dont you pass the shadow of this post"; and Charles replying: "I am going to pass it, Henry." Afterwards, Wash Jones rode up to Miss Rosa's door and yelled until she opened it and then announced in the same tone: "Henry has done shot that durn French feller. Kilt him dead as a beef" (*AA*, 132–33).

A week after Judith buried Bon, she brought to Quentin's grandmother a letter that she said she had received from Bon just before he returned from the war. Although the letter was not addressed to Judith and was not signed by Bon—Ellen Schoenberg argues it was probably intended for the mistress in New Orleans—Mr. Compson believes that this letter, unlike the flowery formal effusions sent from Oxford before the war, proves that Bon loved Judith. Mr. Compson is convinced that Henry saw the letter, and its sincere tone was all the proof he needed to persuade him that Bon was going through with the wedding.

These are the essential facts Quentin has of the Sutpen story when he accompanies Rosa Coldfield out to the old decayed mansion on that September evening of 1909. On their journey out that evening, Miss Rosa says that when she learned that Henry had killed Charles, she went immediately to the Sutpen place. She brushed past Clytie (Judith's black half-sister) and found Judith standing in the door holding in her hand a photograph that she had given Bon. (She also says that she never saw Bon alive.) Seven months later, Sutpen returned, and three months after his return, he and Rosa were engaged. Then one day there was the "death of hope and love, of pride and principle, . . . the death of everything." Sutpen returned to the house and spoke the "outrageous words exactly as if he were

The Role of Quentin Compson in Absalom, Absalom!

consulting with Jones . . . about a bitch dog or a cow or mare" (*AA*, 168). As Shreve will summarize Sutpen's conversation later: He suggested that "they breed together for test and sample and if it was a boy they would marry" (*AA*, 177). As already indicated, after this conversation Miss Rosa returned to Jefferson, not to see Sutpen's Hundred again for more than forty years. Nearly sixty at the time Rosa left, Sutpen made one last desperate effort to save his design. He seduced Wash Jones's granddaughter, but when she bore him a girl he insulted her—saying to the girl that if she were a mare he could give her a warm stall in the barn. Jones killed Sutpen, his grandchild, and her baby, and was himself later killed by the sheriff's posse.

These final details of Sutpen's career—the authorial presence breaks his customary pattern of not intruding into his narrative to tell us that most of Rosa's remarks on Sutpen are highly subjective—are lost on Quentin because he can't get beyond "that door" behind which Bon lay. He imagines Henry "with his shaggy bayonet-trimmed hair, his gaunt worn unshaven face, his patched and faded gray tunic, the pistol still hanging against his flank: the two of them, brother and sister, curiously alike as if the difference in sex had merely sharpened the common blood to a terrific, an almost unbearable, similarity." Always active, Quentin's fertile imagination allows him to hear Henry's remark to his sister: "Now you cant marry him . . . because . . . I killed him" (*AA*, 172).

We have few facts relating the manner in which Quentin spent his time at Harvard during the fall of 1909. Indeed we next see him on a railway siding in Virginia on his way home for Christmas. He gives an old Negro a quarter as a Christmas gift and tells him he'll be back that way "two days after New Year" (*SF*, 107). We don't even get the details of Quentin's and Miss Rosa's visit to Sutpen's Hundred until January, 1910, when Shreve and Quentin are discussing a letter from Mr. Compson in which he relates that Miss Rosa was buried on January 10, after having lain in a coma for two weeks. Knowing Quentin's highly emotional state, however, we can well imagine that during that fall he might have done considerable brooding over what happened to the Sutpen family and why. In fact, some of the highly suggestive conclusions he urges on Shreve regarding the strange behavior of the Sutpens suggest that by January,

1910, he has already arrived at solutions to some of that family's problems that are considerably different from those Mr. Compson had offered. A young man who is utterly confused about his feelings toward his own sister must have found Mr. Compson's speculations about the Bon-Judith-Henry triangle very provocative indeed. For example, there is Mr. Compson's attempt to understand the precise nature of the Judith-Bon relationship: "You see? there they are: this girl ... who sees a man for an average of one hour a day for twelve days during his life and that over a period of a year and a half, yet is bent on marrying him to the extent of forcing her brother to the last resort of homicide" (*AA*, 99). Mr. Compson can no more understand this relationship than Quentin can those Caddy had with Dalton Ames and her other lovers. "Did you love them?" Quentin asked her. "When they touched me," she replied, "I died" (*SF*, 186). Mr. Compson can only offer an explanation which he himself would not accept from Quentin. He would not believe Quentin had had an incestuous affair with Caddy; yet he says, "It ... [was] Henry who seduced Judith, not Bon" (*AA*, 99). We know, of course, that Mr. Compson is not speaking literally in his reference to Judith and Henry, but in his highly distraught emotional state, Quentin cannot be expected to make the necessary figurative leap. Later, as we know, he does confuse Gerald Bland, an acquaintance at Harvard, and Dalton Ames, Caddy's lover.

Mr. Compson's comments about Judith and Henry sound remarkably similar to those he makes in his discussion with Quentin regarding Caddy's promiscuity. To Quentin, referring to Caddy, he says: "it was men invented virginity ... women [are] so delicate so mysterious. ... Delicate equilibrium of periodical filth between two moons balanced. ... People ... cannot do anything very dreadful at all they cannot even remember tomorrow what seemed dreadful today" (*SF*, 96, 159–60, 98). Referring to Henry's attitude toward Judith, he says: Henry may have known "that his fierce provincial's pride in his sister's virginity was a false quantity which must incorporate in itself an inability to endure in order to be precious, to exist, and so must depend upon its loss, absence, to have existed at all. In fact, perhaps this is the pure and perfect incest: the brother realizing that the sister's virginity must be destroyed in order to have existed at all, taking that virginity in the person of the brother-in-law, the man he would be if he could become, metamorphose into, the lover, the husband" (*AA*, 96).

Quentin and Shreve are motivated by Mr. Compson's letter announcing Rosa's death to attempt to flesh out the skeleton of the Sutpen legend that they know. Shreve is having to do the job with less than Quentin's complete participation because Quentin still cannot pass the door where Judith was standing when Henry came to tell her that he had killed Charles Bon. His mind is filled with an image of the brother and sister slashing at each other "with twelve or fourteen words and most of these the same words repeated two or three times so that when you boiled it down they did it with eight or ten" (*AA*, 174). Quentin's fatally wounded psyche is totally involved in the story of the Sutpen children because it includes both parts of his divided self. In his confused emotional state—one in which he cannot define exactly his feelings toward his sister Caddy—he is attracted to Charles Bon, the brother-seducer. And living always with the knowledge of his shameful behavior when he attempted to defend the family's honor by confronting Dalton Ames on the bridge, he must find much to admire in Henry Sutpen, the brother-avenger. In his attempt to bring his sister's seducer to justice, Quentin has been completely humiliated. First Dalton Ames intercepted the blows that Quentin had aimed at his chin— he had held both of Quentin's hands in one of his—then Quentin fainted, and Dalton had lied to him and Caddy, saying he had struck Quentin, in order to help Quentin save face. Surely Quentin's interest in the Sutpen family is partially motivated by his subconscious search for self-respect.

In this mood, then, Quentin tells Shreve on that cold January night in Cambridge, Massachusetts, of his visit to the Sutpen home the previous September and of how he had met Henry Sutpen, who had come home to die. Shreve and Quentin consider Mr. Compson's account of Miss Rosa's visit to the old plantation with an ambulance to bring Henry into town for medical attention. They are aware, too, that Clytie has mistaken the purpose of this visit, thinking the sheriff is coming for Henry; therefore she has set fire to the decayed old house, she and Henry perishing in the flames. The only thing left, then, of Sutpen's design is an idiot black boy "to lurk around those ashes and those four gutted chimneys and howl" until someone comes and drives him away (*AA*, 376).

Together Shreve and Quentin—Faulkner says it might have been either of them speaking and was in a sense both—try to supply some of the missing details in the Sutpen story and to give rational explanations for some of the actions that seem on the surface inexplicable. Quentin's interest in the Judith-Charles-Henry triangle has already been referred to, and Shreve apparently would like to tie up some of the loose ends of a fabulous legend that could have occurred only in that faraway Southland that never existed anywhere at anytime except in his imagination. His view of art is that of the classicist; he is seeking artistic unity, to make all of the details fit a preconceived pattern. Among the many missing details that he and Quentin supply through pure speculation are: that Sutpen told Henry that Charles was his brother but that Charles was not aware of this fact; that there was a lawyer in New Orleans maneuvering events so that Charles went to school at the University of Mississippi in order to meet Henry and, through him, Sutpen; that the lawyer wrote Henry, Henry showed the letter to Bon, and Bon guessed that they were brothers; that Charles merely wanted a hint of recognition from his father; that Henry wrestled with the problem of incest and asked Bon "must you marry our sister?"; that Sutpen told Henry that Charles Bon's mother was part Negro.

This last point is a very important one. In spite of the arguments by Olga Vickery, Cleanth Brooks, and others, there is nowhere in the novel convincing evidence that Bon was part Negro. As Ellen Schoenberg has suggested, the conviction that Charles Bon is part Negro is based on the belief that if this supposition were true it would logically explain why Sutpen put aside his first wife. A Southern white man wanting to be an aristocratic planter in the 1830s would know that a woman of mixed blood could not possibly fit into his "design." But as reasonable as this explanation for Sutpen's action is, the truth of the matter is that this supposition usually accepted as truth was created in Quentin's imagination. If indeed it is a fact, it is one that only Quentin knows, and there is no place he could have learned it—not from his father because his father does not know it; not from his grandfather because there is no evidence that Quentin ever spoke to his grandfather about the Sutpen family; not from Henry Sutpen because, despite Cleanth Brooks's insistence, it is highly unlikely that Quentin's one brief meeting with Henry occurred under conditions that would have made the passing of such information possible. One can only conclude that this bit of crucial information came from the disturbed imagination of Quentin Compson, and the inevitable question, therefore, is why?

In his confused state—one, as I have already said, in which he is both Charles Bon and Henry Sutpen—he can well understand the Charles Bon side of his personality. Unable to understand his own feeling toward his sister—his apparent impotence will not allow him to know for certain the nature of his love for Caddy—he can easily entertain the possibility that one might want to marry his own sister. But why would he kill a brother whom he loves more than anyone else in the world, except to protect the honor of this beloved sister?

To put this matter in proper perspective, one should look again at the famous branch scene of *The Sound and the Fury*. In this, perhaps the central episode in the novel, Caddy wet her dress playing in the branch, and Versh, a young Negro boy a few years older than Caddy, says, "Your mommer going to whip you for getting your dress wet." Caddy replies, "She's not going to do any such thing." And in the ensuing argument, she says she will pull her dress off and let it dry. Quentin tells her she had better not; "You just take your dress off," he warns her. Caddy makes Versh unbutton the dress and she draws it over her head and throws it on the bank to dry, leaving her wearing only her "bodice and drawers." Quentin is so infuriated that Caddy has exposed her body to Versh, a black man, that he "slapped her and . . . she fell down in the water" (*SF*, 19–20).

Shreve is closer than he knows to expressing Quentin's deepest concerns, therefore, when he says that maybe one day in the spring following the Christmas visit Bon merely concluded, "All right I want to go to bed with a girl who might be my sister." After the four years in the war have settled nothing, Bon must have decided, Shreve and Quentin conclude, definitely to go back and marry Judith. In a scene much like that with Dalton Ames at the bridge—and one created by Quentin's disturbed imagination—Charles hands Henry a pistol and tells him to shoot him if he wishes to prevent the wedding. In Quentin's version, Henry is as inept as he was himself at the bridge; Henry's hand trembles as he looks at the pistol: "You are my brother," he says. "No I'm not," Bon responds. "I'm the nigger that's going to sleep with your sister. Unless you stop me." This remark arouses Henry. In terms of Quentin's own psychic dilemma, the part of him that is the brother-seducer (Charles Bon) is opposed by the part that is the brother-avenger (Henry Sutpen). In the tale he is concocting, Quentin is able in one stroke to chastise the sister who would expose herself to a black man and to bring to justice the man who would despoil that sister. This remark—"I'm the nigger that's going to sleep with your sister"—provokes immediate action: The boys propose that Henry grabs the pistol from Bon, flings it away, grabs Bon by the shoulder and says, "You shall not! You shall not! Do you hear me?" Bon responds, "You will have to stop me, Henry"; and they begin the long ride back to Sutpen's Hundred (*AA*, 357–58). When they arrive at the gate and Charles still has not changed his mind, Quentin imagines Henry, with his pistol lying unaimed across his saddle bow, saying: *"Dont you pass the shadow of this post."* (Quentin's ultimatum to Dalton Ames: "Be out of town before sundown.") When Bon passes the shadow, Henry, as Wash Jones says, shoots him "dead as a beef." Then the boy who cannot bear to see his sister strip before their black companion imagines Henry rushing up to his sister, who is threatened with ravishment by a Negro, yelling, "Now you cant marry him . . . because . . . I killed him" (*AA*, 133, 172).

To comprehend the harrowing tale Quentin and Shreve have created out of the sparse set of facts at their disposal, one must always be mindful of Shreve's lack of knowledge of the South. To him it is a not-quite-real kind of place, one in which the fantastic, Gothic legend he and Quentin have concocted could have and probably did occur. But for Quentin the tale is of another quality and serves a different function. A highly disturbed, psychotic personality desperately seeking a solution to the psychic dilemma that threatens to strangle him, he is, I repeat, mentally ill, and like all persons similarly affected, he cannot escape his own set of mental facts. Quentin can relate to Henry Sutpen, however, because Henry is able to avenge a great wrong that threatens his sister. We must realize, however, that the Henry

Sutpen of fact, the one who lived near Jefferson and attended the University of Mississippi, is not the Henry Sutpen that Quentin has created. The real Henry Sutpen undoubtedly was able to place in proper perspective and accept, therefore, an escalating series of Old South taboos: bigamy, bigotry, miscegenation, and maybe even incest. He is sane, if somewhat naïve, and is consequently intensely affected by the attitudes of his society. Quentin, on the other hand, is deeply disturbed and therefore is not rational. Because of the ambiguous nature of his own feeling toward Caddy, he can understand why a man might have erotic desires for his own sister. In his disturbed state, however, he associates promiscuity with miscegenation, which to many in the Old South was promiscuity carried to its most horrible extreme. To fulfill his deepest need, therefore, Quentin creates a Henry who is able to tolerate Bon's marrying his own sister but who is unable to accept the overt promiscuity of a black man sleeping with that beloved sister.

Shreve has fashioned a tale with enough suspense and melodrama to do justice to his conception of the South, a land in which, as he expressed it, "it takes two niggers to get rid of one Sutpen." And in the fullness of time he says the Jim Bonds "are going to conquer the western hemisphere." Quentin is not listening too closely, for his interest is not really in Jim Bond, except maybe as his irrational howling reminds him of the sound his brother Benjy makes. When Shreve asks, however, "Why do you hate the South?" Quentin responds in utter frustration, "I dont! I dont hate it! I dont hate it!" (*AA*, 378). For the story Quentin creates and assists Shreve in articulating is only indirectly about the South, and he thinks Shreve has missed the point of his tale. What Quentin is really trying to sort out is precisely how he feels about his sister Caddy and what kind of response his confused emotional state will permit him to make. His is a tale born of desperation. Perhaps his opportunity to create a story detailing the circumstances under which an incestuous love of brother for sister is at least quasi-acceptable—and at the same time to create his alter ego, a character powerful enough to punish his sister's would-be seducer—provides Quentin strength to get through the last torturous year of his life. We see him only twice more: in April, when he returns to Jefferson to attend Caddy's wedding (when he is a rather assertive, effective young man, getting T. P. and Benjy, who have had too much champagne, out of the front yard and into the barn); and on June 2 as he executes a careful, meticulously prepared plan for his own death by leaping from a bridge much like the one upon which he had humiliated himself before Dalton Ames. His vicarious experience as hero, apparently, could sustain him no longer.

(1976)

Ransom's Critical Theories: Image and Idea

IN the fall of 1937, John Crowe Ransom published "Criticism, Inc.," his best-known critical essay, in which he sets forth what he calls the "proper business of criticism." For too long, he protests, our critics have been amateurs, men without the specific qualifications to perform the highly specialized functions that they have undertaken. The kinds of competence a critic needs could be expected to come from one of three sources, but none of these has produced the sort of precise and systematic criticism needed to permit literature to convey the unique kind of knowledge it possesses.[1] The first group of "trained performers" from which a reader might reasonably expect the kind of assistance that he requires is the artist himself, but results from this source have often been disappointing. The artist is not necessarily a reliable critic, for even though he "should know good art when he sees it," his "understanding is often intuitive rather than dialectical." As long as he sticks to the technical effects of the art works with which he is familiar, his commentary is usually valuable; but often when he attempts to expound a theory of art his critical weaknesses are glaringly apparent. The second source from which sound criticism should derive is the philosopher. But the philosopher, who should know "all about the function of the fine arts," is not always a dependable critic. He is weak where the artist is strong: He can expound a theory of art, but he is usually not well enough acquainted with individual works to comment on specific technical effects.[2]

This essay originally appeared, in slightly different form, in *The New Criticism and After*, ed. Thomas Daniel Young (Charlottesville, Va., 1976). Reprinted by permission of the University of Virginia Press.

1. John Crowe Ransom, "Criticism, Inc.," in Ransom, *The World's Body* (New York, 1938), 327.
2. *Ibid.*, 327–28.

Since the reader of poetry can get the kind of critical assistance that he needs from neither the artist nor the philosopher, to whom should he turn? The logical source of the kind of help he needs and deserves is the university professor of English. But those readers who look to the universities for this kind of help, Ransom warns, will surely be disappointed. The professors of English are "learned but not critical men"; it would seem that they have "appropriated every avenue of escape from their responsibility" that is either decent or official. They spend a lifetime compiling the "data of literature" and rarely if ever commit themselves to a literary judgment. Some of them are good textual, philological, and historical scholars, but few can or will provide the precise and systematic criticism the work of art demands. Ransom calls, therefore, for a Criticism, Incorporated, in order that this important activity may be "taken in hand by professionals."[3]

This essay has often been cited as the clarion call for the New Criticism, an appeal for a new approach to literary study, for criticism concerned with formal analysis and literary judgments, with the insights that come only from an intensive study of the poem itself. Obviously, Ransom is defining the kind of criticism that he thought absolutely essential if literature is to retain a significant role in the life of civilized man. But it was not a new criticism. He merely defined formally the approach to literature that he himself had been advocating and practicing for more than twenty years when this essay appeared.

In February, 1914, he had outlined in a letter to his father a theory of poetics, which he had worked out in many conversations with Samuel C. Chew, who at that time was his colleague on the faculty of the Hotchkiss School in Lakeville, Connecticut. In the teaching of Latin poetry, Ransom wrote his father, he was able to recognize a good translation of Virgil, because the translation is poetry, even if it does not contain meter. Although everyone would admit that poetry in its most nearly complete form employs meter, what else it contains has not been formulated, and the best place to study this question is in a good translation of the poetry of another language. If one sets out to determine how a translation that "satisfies good taste" differs from

3. *Ibid.*

"correct and formal" prose, he will make several interesting discoveries. He will find, first of all, that the "good translation preserves the discontinuities, ellipses, the failing to attain preciseness and perfect connection" because the "mode of thought that is imaginative rather than logical or scientific" is induced through the use of words "which mean the given thing yet involve it in accidental associations that provoke the imagination." Even the meter is calculated to induce the imaginative rather than the logical mode because words "have a double nature: They stand for things and are associated inseparably with thought." Although in prose the author may be unconscious of the sound of his words, in poetry he provides a musical arrangement of words within which is fitted as much of the intended meaning as possible. The musical requirement, however, is usually so restrictive that the choice of words to convey the meaning is severely limited; therefore the poet must deploy words "which fail of precision and introduce extraneous color and distract the attention and suggest beautiful enterprises of the imagination." As soon as he could develop his poetic theory in detail, Ransom concluded, he hoped to demonstrate that there is an "inevitable union between poetic form and what is called poetic imagination."[4]

During the fall and winter of 1913–1914, almost ten years before his first essay in literary theory appeared, Ransom's basic concept of the nature and function of the poetic structure was already fixed in his mind. This rudimentary discussion of the dual role of words in the poetic translation anticipates by more than twenty years his definition of the poem, in "Wanted: An Ontological Critic" (1941), as a "loose logical structure with a good deal of local texture." The poem may be differentiated from the prose discourse on the basis of this "odd structure." Over the years, he would attempt to designate exactly how the poem "differs from the prose discourse." It is, he insisted more than once, an *order* rather than a *kind* of content that "distinguishes texture from structure and poetry from prose." The differentia of poetry as discourse is an ontological one; its nature differs from that of the prose discourse because it serves a different purpose. The suggestion presented in this early letter—that

---

4. Thomas Daniel Young and George Core (eds.), *Selected Letters of John Crowe Ransom* (Baton Rouge, 1985), 86.

poetry attempts to "induce the mode of thought that is *imaginative* rather than logical"—is an obvious, if an incomplete and inexact statement of his defense of poetry as a means of cognition, not of instruction. "Poetry intends," he wrote in 1941, near the middle of his career, "to recover the denser and more refractory original world which we know loosely through our perceptions and memories." It is "ontologically distinct" because it is the "kind of knowledge by which we must know what we have arranged that we shall not know otherwise."[5]

These two concepts, the foundation upon which almost all of his later aesthetic speculation was based, were extracted, Ransom later admitted, from Aristotle, Plato, Plautus, Kant, Hegel, Schopenhauer, and Coleridge, some of the thinkers whom he had studied regularly since his undergraduate days at Vanderbilt and particularly at Oxford, where he had read the Greats. These ideas were first formulated and given tentative expression in conversations with the members of the Hermit Crabs, a literary club he had organized at Oxford in 1911. In the discussions with Samuel Chew, who had diverted his attention from the classics to English literature, they began to assume the basic form in which they would be published many years later. His first real interest in literary theorizing, which began in 1913, the year he taught at the Hotchkiss School, was stimulated so much by his associations with Allen Tate, Donald Davidson, and the other Fugitives at Vanderbilt that by the mid-1920s, criticism was claiming the major part of his creative energies. During the last year of its existence, the *Fugitive*, which was published in Nashville from 1922 to 1925, provided him the opportunity to express for publication some of the critical ideas that had been slowly evolving over the past ten or more years. In the first of these essays, Ransom presents in essence the views that would comprise the introduction to *The World's Body*, published nearly fifteen years later. "The respectable attainments of much recent poetry," he wrote in "Mixed Modes" (March, 1925), "exist to controvert the view that poets are essentially juveniles." Such a view, he insisted, might have been entertained in 1900, at the close of a century of

---

5. John Crowe Ransom, "Wanted: An Ontological Critic," in Ransom, *The New Criticism* (Norfolk, Conn., 1941), 280–81; Young and Core (eds.), *Selected Letters of John Crowe Ransom*, 86; Ransom, *The World's Body*, x.

the simplest poetry in English literary history, but this is not *the* literary tradition. For the real literary tradition one must go back beyond the "nonsense melodies of Swinburne," the "sinister naiveté of the pre-Raphaelites," even further back than Tennyson, Browning, and the English romantic poets, to the time when a poet could "devote a complete act of cerebration to each of his poetical themes," to the age of Chaucer, Spenser, Shakespeare, and Milton, when the poet could "put his whole mind and experience to work in poetry." If poetry is to be the kind of activity that will engage the mind of an adult, he concludes, it cannot be the "paregoric of lullaby." The poets "must report their own mixed modes," not attempt "to simplify and prettify the theme." They must produce a kind of poetry, as Ransom said in *The World's Body* (1938), that will appeal to persons who have aged in the "pure intellectual disciplines" and cannot "play innocent without feeling very foolish."[6]

Two other essays published in the *Fugitive* later the same year demonstrate quite clearly that by the mid-1920s Ransom was very near to establishing critical positions he would never abandon. In "Thoughts on the Poetic Discontent" (June, 1925), he sets up the conflict between science and art by suggesting some of the differences between the knowledge acquired by the scientific method and the knowledge resulting from an analytical study of poetry and the other arts. This brief note not only contains a clear statement of this basic distinction, one essential in the evolution of his mature theories, but it includes as well the germ of some of his most sophisticated critical concepts. In his intellectual development, Ransom suggests early in this essay, man moves through three stages. Beginning as a dualist, aware both of the "world without and the spirit within," he proceeds through a period of monism (in which he attempts to set up a mystical union with God and nature) before he reaches a third stage, one in which a reaffirmation of dualism occurs. But now he is a "dualist with a difference"; he possesses a "mellow wisdom which we may call irony." This state "presupposes the others" because it implies a "strenuous period of romantic creation" and then a rejection of all romantic forms. But this rejection is nei-

---

6. John Crowe Ransom, "Mixed Modes," *Fugitive*, IV (March, 1925), 29; Ransom, *The World's Body*, viii.

ther easy nor complete; it is arrived at so unwillingly that there "lingers ... much of the music and color and romantic mystery which is perhaps the absolute poetry." In the second essay, "Prose: A Doctrine of Relativity" (September, 1925), he argues that a poem has many meanings. In addition to its fable, which often is not as innocent as it looks, there may be dozens of words and phrases to lead the mind away from the poem's logical content and into seemingly irrelevant excursions. But here the differences between poetry and scientific discourse become apparent. Poetry uses the "widest terms" possible, science the narrowest; and these terms "function precisely to evoke in our memories the deepest previous experience." Thus poetry is art, not science; and its reference is "always free and personal," never "fixed and ideal."[7]

During the late 1920s, then, Ransom was working toward the complete articulation of the aesthetic principles upon which he would establish his ontological theory of criticism. During these years, he was engaged in an important correspondence with Allen Tate that allowed him to test and refine his artistic speculations under the penetrating scrutiny of one of the most active critical minds of the twentieth century. In a letter written in December, 1923, as a part of his explanation of why he found the poetry of T. S. Eliot difficult, Ransom again attempted to describe the unique nature of the art object:

> The art-thing sounds like the first immediate transcript of reality, but it isn't; it's a long way from the event. It isn't the raw stuff of experience. The passion in it has mellowed down—emotion recollected in *tranquility*, etc. Above all things else, the core of experience in the record has been taken up into the sum total of things and its relations there discovered are given in the works of art. That is why the marginal meanings, the associations, the interlinear element of a poem are all-important. The most delicate piece of work that a poet has to do is to avoid a misleading connection in his phrasing. There must not be a trace of the expository philosophical method, but nevertheless the substance of the philosophical conclusion must be there for the intelligent reader.[8]

7. John Crowe Ransom, "Thoughts on the Poetic Discontent," *Fugitive*, IV (June, 1925), 63–64; Ransom, "Prose: A Doctrine of Relativity," *Fugitive*, IV (September, 1925), 93.

8. John Crowe Ransom to Allen Tate, December, 1923, in Jesse E. Wills Fugitive/Agrarian Collection, Special Collections, Jean and Alexander Heard Library, Vanderbilt University.

In addition to an apparent effort to express what he will later call the structure-texture formulation of the poem, one can detect in this statement an interest in identifying the unique characteristics of the poetic structure through an examination of the creative process itself.

By the late 1920s, Ransom was convinced that the ideas that had been slowly surfacing for almost a decade had developed sufficiently to require an extensive essay to give them adequate expression; consequently, he spent the better part of a year on an essay that he called "The Third Moment." After months of almost uninterrupted writing, he completed a manuscript of two hundred pages, which during the next several years he revised many times, trying to get it in shape for publication. Finally he decided that it was hopelessly abstract, that such a study could be "pursued only in the constant company of the actual poems"; therefore, as he said ten years later, he "had the pleasure of consigning it to the flames."[9] Since no copy of this manuscript exists, its contents must be reconstructed from the letters that Ransom wrote Allen Tate during the period of its composition. On September 5, 1926, he discussed in some detail what he was trying to do. There are, this letter begins, "three moments in the historical order of experience": the first is the actual experience itself, "pure of all intellectual content, unreflective, concrete, and singular; there are no distinctions and the subject is identical with the whole." In the second moment "cognition takes place," and a record must be made of the first moment. This record is made by way of "*concepts* discovered in cognition." This is the beginning of science with its intent upon practicality and its compulsion to produce abstractions through subtracting parts from the whole experience. Only in the third moment are we "aware of the deficiency of the record"; only then do we realize that "most of [the] experience is quite missing from it." All "our concepts" and "all our histories" combined can never restore the whole experience. That "fugitive first moment" can be recovered only through images; it cannot be reproduced through philosophical synthesis:

> How can we get back to that first moment? There is only one answer: By images. The Imagination is the faculty of Pure Memory, or unconscious mind; it brings out the original experiences from the dark

9. Ransom, *The World's Body*, vii.

storeroom, where we dwell upon them with a joy proportionate to our previous despair. And therefore, when we make images, we are regressive; we are trying to reconstitute an experience which we once had, only to handle and mutilate. Only, we cannot quite reconstitute them. Association is too strong for us; the habit of cognition is too strong. The images come out mixed and adulterated with concepts. . . . [W]e are not really opposed to science, except as it monopolises and warps us; we are perfectly content to dwell in the phenomenal world for much of our time; this is to be specifically human; we would not be babes nor beasts; we require merely the fulness of life, which is existence in the midst of all our faculties.

Man tries, then, to reconstitute the elusive first moment in all its concrete particularity through fancies (or daydreams), dreams, religion, morals, and art. Ransom concludes this lengthy explication of his theory by offering again his definition of poetry, this time calling it the "exhibit of Opposition and at the same time Reconciliation between the Conceptual or Formal and the Individual or Concrete."[10] This is his earliest statement of his concept of the Concrete Universal, which is developed in two essays in the mid-1950s and in his last published essay, written in 1970.

The "obvious fact," he wrote to Tate, which years before had started him on this line of inquiry, was his realization that the requirement of meter in poetry, "an undeniable example of the Formal, does not seem to impair the life and effectiveness of Concrete Experience. They coexist."[11] Here he could well be referring to the speculation that preceded the letter he had written his father nearly fifteen years before. Based upon the summary given in the letter to Tate, in "The Third Moment" Ransom proposed to include many of the critical ideas that in fact did not receive formal expression until the publication of the well-known essays of the thirties, forties, and fifties: that aesthetic theory should have a firm ontological basis; that the material object is the "stuff" of poetry, that the essential nature of poetry resides in its dualism; that the poem can reconstitute the "fugitive first moment," the world's body, through a combination of concept and image; that the view of human experience presented by science, with its practical ends and abstract means, is less than complete; that human experience can be fully realized only through art.

10. Young and Core (eds.), *Selected Letters of John Crowe Ransom*, 156.
11. *Ibid.*, 157.

During the 1930s and 1940s, Ransom made many attempts to define that "precious object," which can restore the concrete particularities of the world's body if one will meditate it properly—that is, if he is impelled "neither to lay hands on the object immediately nor to ticket it for tomorrow's outrage but to conceive [of] it as having its own existence." To know a work of art one must be capable of an aesthetic experience; he must entertain what Schopenhauer called "knowledge without desire." In the preface to *The World's Body,* Ransom indicates that the post-scientific poetry to which he and his generation are attached is the "act of a fallen mind," a poetry that attempts to "realize the world," not to "idealize it." Modern man has little knowledge of the world in which he lives except that which is revealed through scientific observation. His conception of the world is faulty because it is incomplete. To view the world only in the manner of the scientist is to fail to realize its body and solid substance. If we are to know the world, "which is made of whole and indefeasible objects," we must recover it through poetry from our memory to which it has retired.[12] Poetry, then, is an order of knowledge quite distinct from that which one achieves through science, and it is the only means through which one can know the concrete particularity of the world's body. This argument is an obvious extension of the line of speculation that Ransom had been engaged in more than ten years before when he tried to identify and define, in the letter to Tate, the "three moments" that comprise the historical order of experience. In his view, the only way in which the actual experience can be recovered in its totality is through art, dreams, or religious myth. The record made in the "second moment," by scientists and social scientists, is formed through the process of subtracting from the whole, by formulating concepts and abstract ideas derived from concentration on one aspect of the whole. When man realizes that his record of the experience is only a partial one, he may also understand that the elusive first moment can never be recovered through abstract speculation or philosophical syntheis. If he resorts to poetry as the means through which the experience is reconstituted, he must deal with a mixed world, one composed of both ideas and images.

Ransom's continued interest in this mixed world led him, in

---

12. Ransom, *The World's Body,* viii, x.

some of his most influential essays, to discuss the nature and function of poetry, to differentiate among its several types, and to contrast its aims and purposes with those of science. As he covers again this now very familiar ground, it becomes abundantly clear that there is no fundamental change in his critical position. What seems a major shift of belief or opinion is usually an attempt to clarify a misunderstood statement by supplying additional details or, as is often the case, by changing his metaphor.

In "Poetry: A Note in Ontology" (1934), he defines and ranks three kinds of poetry. The first is physical poetry, the mode that the Imagists produced, which intends to "present things in their thingness," and in this intention is diametrically opposed to "that poetry which dwells as firmly as it dares upon ideas." The image, Ransom argues, "cannot be dispossessed of primordial freshness, which idea can never claim." The image is in its "natural or wild state," where it has to be discovered; it is not made by man and operates according to the laws of its own nature. Man cannot "lay hold of [an] image and take it captive," as he can an idea, which Ransom defines as the "image with its character beaten out of it." Science can destroy the image, not as some think—through refutation—but by taming it and destroying its freedom through abstraction. Through the use of the so-called scientific method, man can weaken his imagination to the extent that he can no longer "contemplate things as they are in their rich and contingent materiality." As he had argued repeatedly over the years in his correspondence with Tate and others, Ransom insists that man is compelled to poetry through memory and dream; it follows, therefore, that art is "based on second love, not first love." Through it, man attempts to return to something he has lost, to capture that elusive first moment, the experience itself in all its rich particularity. Ransom values physical poetry because it attempts to go beyond the abstractions of science by constant recourse to image, but this kind of poetry reproduces only a part of the experience. To reconstitute the total experience requires a combination of image and idea.[13]

If physical poetry is a "half poetry," the second mode, Platonic poetry, is "bogus poetry." It tries to pose as the real thing by hiding its ideas behind its images, but its images can always be

13. John Crowe Ransom, "Poetry: A Note in Ontology," *ibid.*, 113–16.

translated into ideas as if to prove that nature is rational and can be possessed through logic. The Platonic poet does not accept the basic principle of "the third moment": the world of ideas is not the original world of perception; therefore, the whole and comprehensible object cannot be presented through logical statement. The original world of perception, the first moment, must be "experienced, and cannot be reported." Through his false poetry the Platonist attempts to demonstrate that "an image will prove an idea," and his images are employed merely as illustrations of ideas. At this point in the essay, Ransom reiterates an argument first presented many years earlier. Man must "recant from his Platonism and turn back to things" if he would restore to poetry some of the vigor and strength that it once possessed; but as he turns from his idealizing, he must be fully aware of how deeply he has been affected by his excursion into Platonism. In "Thoughts on the Poetic Discontent," he had argued that man's mature attitude is tempered by irony and poetry, because he is reluctant to give up "the music and color" and the "romantic mystery" of his belief in the existence of a "mystical community," a union between subject and object, percept and concept, man and nature. This idea is restated now in different language. Man's withdrawal from Platonism is neither easy nor complete. From this dualistic state, in which he is pulled in two directions simultaneously, comes the complex attitude which produces the aesthetic moment: an instant of "suspension . . . between the Platonism in us, which is militant, always sciencing and devouring, and a starved inhibited aspiration towards innocence" which would like to "know the object as it might . . . reveal itself." Thus the "poetic impulse is not free." Because it means to reconstitute the world of perception, it stubbornly resists the pressures of science in order to enjoy its images. From this "adult mode" in which images and ideas vie for the attention of the mature man comes true poetry, and poetry is produced in that "curious moment of suspension" in which the imagination attempts to reconstitute an experience that we have allowed to become mutilated, abstracted, and universalized by the scientists, the social scientists, and the philosophers.[14]

Out of this "mixed and complex" world comes true poetry.

14. *Ibid.*, 128, 130; Ransom, "Thoughts on the Poetic Discontent," 64.

Here Ransom characterizes this "true poetry" as metaphysical poetry, though he admitted in a letter to Tate before the essay was published that the term was too specialized and restrictive. A distinguishing characteristic of this poetry is its use of the conceit, which Ransom says is a "meant metaphor," one which is "developed so literally that it must be good" or "predicated so baldly that nothing else can be meant." In this metaphorical assertion, a "miraculism" or "supernaturalism" occurs if the poet not only means what he says but compels the reader to believe what he has read. This miraculism comes as the result of the poet's having discovered "by analogy an identity between objects which is partial, though it should be considerable, and proceeds to an identification which is complete." From this kind of miraculism, poetry derives its ontological significance because it makes available an order of knowledge that one can get from no other source. For it is "the poet and nobody else who gives to God a nature, a form, faculties, and a history." Without poetry to give God a body and a solid substance, He "would remain the driest and deadest among Platonic ideas." Myths are "conceits, born of metaphors," and religions are "produced by poets and destroyed by naturalists."[15]

In 1941, Ransom admitted that even after years of dedicated effort he had been unable to find the fusion of thought and feeling that T. S. Eliot had attributed to some of the poets who had lived in the seventeenth century and earlier. He was convinced, he said, that a thought cannot be felt; nevertheless a thought can be and often is conducted simultaneously with "irrelevant feelings." The unique phenomenon which Eliot described can best be presented, Ransom insisted, by what he called his structure-texture formulation, the well-known and often contested phrase he devised to delineate the essential duality of poetry. The reader of a poem, Ransom argues in *The New Criticism* (1941), can realize the *structure*, which is the logical thought, without sacrificing *texture*, which is the free detail, or "the feelings that engage in the free detail." Eliot's affective language can be translated, then, into the objective or cognitive terms which Ransom had developed over twenty-five years. Eliot's "big emotion" is attached to the "main thought" or the "logical structure" of the poem at the

---

15. Ransom, "Poetry: A Note in Ontology," 139–40.

same time the "little feelings" are evoked by the "play of the words" or the local texture.[16]

Here Ransom is still attempting to point up the differences between the poetic and the scientific structures, and he insists that this differentiation cannot be made on the basis of "moralism," "emotionalism," or "sensibility," for all of these are conducted very well in prose. The unique nature of poetry can be identified only by its odd structure, whose exact purpose is difficult to describe. It is a structure not "so tight and precise on its logical side as a scientific or prose structure generally is" but one that "imports and carries along a great deal of irrelevant or foreign matter which is clearly not structural but even obstructive." What makes this statement significant is Ransom's insistence that poetry is knowledge because it includes a content which, though of a *kind* similar to that of prose, is of a vastly different *order*. Poetry "treats an order of existence, a grade of objectivity," which cannot be treated in scientific discourse.

The difference between poetry and scientific prose, then, is basically an ontological one; only through poetry can man recover the "body and solid substance of the world." The basic kind of data which science can collect reduces the world to a "scheme of abstract conveniences." Science is interested only in *knowing*, but art has a double function: it wants both to *know* and to *make*. Because their intentions vary so widely, science and art employ different kinds of signs to communicate their discoveries and conclusions: science uses mere symbols, whose only function is to refer to some other object, but art uses icons, which not only refer to other objects but "resemble or imitate those objects." The object symbolized by the scientific sign is an abstraction or a single property of the object represented, but that suggested by the aesthetic sign or icon is the whole object.

After the publication of "Wanted: An Ontological Critic" in 1941, Ransom wrote many essays in which he attempted to demonstrate how the ontological critic should react in his efforts to define the nature of poetic discourse and to justify its existence in a society becoming more and more enamored of the quasi knowledge and the false promises of science. But as effective

---

16. Ransom, "Wanted: an Ontological Critic," 280–81, 294–336. Quotations in the next two paragraphs also are taken from this source.

as these essays have been in convincing many readers that the truths of poetry can be revealed only through a close and analytical study of the text itself, they do not represent an essential change in his critical position. Ransom's "restless exploration of the grounds of criticism," to use Allen Tate's phrase, continued, however, and during the forties and fifties he published a dozen or more essays which demonstrate his preoccupation with the unique nature of poetry.[17] In "Poetry: The Formal Analysis" (1947), he castigates some of his fellow critics for concentrating too much on the poem's texture and neglecting its structure. Some of them, he writes, approach the poem in the manner of the "bee who gathers honey from the several blossoms as he comes to them, without noticing the bush which supports all the blossoms." Because they are "careless of the theoretical constitution of poetry," these critics tend to create an impression of the poem's disorder at the same time that they make the reader aware of many "exciting turns of poetic language."[18]

In these last essays, Ransom covered much of the ground he had been over earlier as he attempts to clear up misunderstood statements or fuzzily expressed concepts. His definition of a poem, however, does not change. Even the language is the same; it remains a "logical structure having a local texture." In "Old Age of an Eagle," he analyzes the three dimensions of a poem: its plot or argument, its meter, and its language. It has an "ostensible argument" that can be rendered in prose and a "tissue of meaning" that cannot. Although a poem is never completely represented in its paraphrase, which always reduces the text, it always includes its own paraphrase, which is both "useful" and "reputable" because it "straightens out the text and prunes meaning down."[19]

In Ransom's three essays on the Concrete Universal, he reiterates his belief that the technical sciences attempt to know the natural world in order to tame it, to reduce it and take what they want from it. Unlike Hegel, who insists that the concrete is wholly

17. Allen Tate, "A Note on Critical 'Autotelism,'" in Tate, *Essays of Four Decades* (Chicago, 1970), 169.
18. John Crowe Ransom, "Poetry: The Formal Analysis," *Kenyon Review*, IX (Summer, 1947), 436.
19. John Crowe Ransom, "Old Age of an Eagle," in Ransom, *Poems and Essays* (New York, 1955), 79.

assimilated in the universal, he follows Kant in arguing that the "concrete detail is partly extraneous to the abstract universal"; for this reason, the complete meaning of a poem can never be expressed in logical terms. Again he attempts to define the unique nature of the poem. His attempt to identify the poem as having a logical structure and an irrelevant texture, he wrote, has worried him because "texture" has come to strike him as "a flat or inadequate figure for that vital and easily felt part of the poem which we associate particularly with poetic language." Now he would say a poem is an "organism," composed of head, heart, and feet.[20] All these organs work together to produce a poem, each speaking in a different language, the head in an intellectual language, the heart in an affective language, and the feet in a rhythmical language. Through appropriate combinations of these three kinds of language, poetry of the right kind can present the concrete universal, only a part of which is included in the scientific discourse. This kind of poetry can assist the reader in knowing the world, for in it the imagination, through metaphor, makes the moral universal, which is abstract and conceptual, concrete and perceptual. The universal is referred to nature and particularized, given sensuous detail through this reference. Thus nature is essential for poetry. To abandon nature is to abandon metaphor. Without metaphor there can be no poetry, and without poetry man's knowledge of himself and his world is fragmentary and incomplete.

(1975)

20. John Crowe Ransom, "The Concrete Universal: Observations on the Understanding of Poetry, I" *Kenyon Review*, XVI (Autumn, 1954), 559.

Ransom's Critical Theories: Structure and Texture

*I*N a brief prefatory statement to *The World's Body* (1938), John Crowe Ransom acknowledges his indebtedness to his old friend Allen Tate:

> I am . . . under obligations to Mr. Allen Tate, with whom I have generally been in close communication, and whose views of poetry I share, so far as I know them, with fewest and slightest reservations. Between us, when the talk was at a certain temperature, I have seen observations come to the surface in a manner to illustrate the theory of anonymous or communal authorship.[1]

This expression of indebtedness to Tate contains a partial description of a procedure that Ransom had found a definite stimulant to his creative imagination. At Oxford, he had helped to form a literary club, the Hermit Crabs, and the discussions there of such authors as Ibsen, Wilde, Stevenson, and Synge turned his attention toward literary criticism. During this period and later, he often found that he could come nearer mastering an idea he was grappling with if he could "argue it out" with a skeptical antagonist. First with his father, then with his friends at Oxford, and later with Samuel Chew at the Hotchkiss School, he had held many animated discussions, which, he found, assisted him enormously in formulating and refining his attitudes on a broad spectrum of literary and philosophical topics. By the mid-1920s, the critical ideas that had been slowly evolving for more than ten years had become so firmly established that he published his first criticism, a series of brief critical statements in the *Fugitive*. In "Mixed Modes," "Thoughts on the Poetic Dis-

---

This essay originally appeared, in slightly different form, in *Mississippi Quarterly*, XXX (Winter, 1976–77). Reprinted by permission of the editor.

1. John Crowe Ransom, *The World's Body* (New York, 1938), xv.

content," and "A Doctrine of Relativity," he first expressed formally some of the basic principles of a theory of aesthetics that would influence a whole generation of critics: that the knowledge available from the proper study of poetry is of an order different from that acquired from science. Only a part of a poem's meaning may be extracted from the logical content of its fable, for much is often contained in the seemingly irrelevant excursions suggested by a word or a phrase. Irony is the ultimate mode of the great minds because it presupposes all the others.[2]

Except for a brief period of alienation resulting from a fundamental disagreement over the merits of *The Waste Land*, Ransom and Tate discussed freely and fully with each other their theories of the nature and function of poetry. Between 1925 and 1928, the two poet-critics engaged in a lively exchange of letters, which allowed both of them to give definite focus and specific form to some of their most significant critical ideas. At this time, Ransom, on leave of absence from Vanderbilt, was attempting to prepare an extensive critical essay, which he had given the working title of "The Third Moment." Ransom destroyed this essay, which he later referred to as a "general aesthetic of poetry, a kind of Prolegomena to Any Future Poetic," because he decided it was too abstract. Such a critical study, he wrote in 1938, "can scarcely afford to be pursued . . . except in the constant company of the actual poems." All was not lost, however, because the fundamentals of that "general aesthetic of poetry," at least as it was outlined in the extensive correspondence with Tate, appeared in *God Without Thunder* (1930) and *The World's Body* (1938).[3]

Soon after *The World's Body* was published, Ransom wrote Tate of his dissatisfaction with the book, particularly with "Poetry: A Note in Ontology," which, he felt, was "a central esssay" in the collection. In that piece—after he had discussed two kinds of "half poetries": 1) physical poetry, "which dwells as exclusively as it dares upon . . . things," and 2) Platonic poetry, "which dwells as firmly as it dares upon ideas"—he comes to the true

2. John Crowe Ransom, "Mixed Modes," *Fugitive*, IV (March, 1925), 28–29; Ransom, "Thoughts on the Poetic Discontent," *Fugitive*, IV (June, 1925), 63–64; Ransom, "Prose: A Doctrine of Relativity," *Fugitive*, IV (September, 1925), 93–94.

3. John Crowe Ransom, "Waste Lands," *Literary Review*, July 14, 1923, pp. 825–26.

poetry, which he calls metaphysical and defines as a kind of poetry containing a "miraculism or supernaturalism in a metaphorical assertion." The miraculism occurs, he says, "when the poet discovers by analogy an identity between objects which is partial, though it should be considerable, and proceeds to an identification which is complete." Before the book was officially released, however, he wrote Tate that the label he had placed on this kind of poetry was too restrictive:

> The Note in Ontology is a central essay, and I'm glad you see it so. Unfortunately, after clearing the ground in my first two sections of it (the Physical and Platonic half-poetries) I don't denominate and define the true exhibit; it should be Integral Poetry, or Molecular Poetry, or True Poetry, or Whole or Organic Poetry, or Absolute Poetry, or something; the Metaphysical Poetry is just a variety, and it's a good variety to exhibit with, but its name should not have preempted the title and the general definition. I rather rode two horses in that essay, or tried to. I think I have the right introductory matter in the last section, in leading up to the Metaphysical style, though I don't advertise it properly. I remember you once wanted the term Creative Poetry, and I demurred a little on the ground of something magical or mystical in the connotation.[4]

Ransom's desire to state precisely his ontological theory of the nature and function of poetry led him to seek other modes of expression, new figures and analogies, that would allow him to indicate the exact differences between the language of science and that of poetry. This search led him to Charles W. Morris' *Foundations of the Theory of Signs*, a book he found so impressive that he urged Tate to read it, calling it "really brilliant" and saying it "makes Richards look mighty small." Tate secured a copy, read it, and wrote Ransom his reactions. The extent to which both critics were influenced by Morris' principles can be seen by reading Tate's "Literature as Knowledge" and Ransom's "Wanted: An Ontological Critic." Although Ransom was delighted, he said, that the scientists and philosophers were not completely neglecting the arts, he was disturbed that neither would accept the simple fact he had been arguing for years: Sci-

---

4. John Crowe Ransom, "Poetry: A Note in Ontology," in Ransom, *The World's Body*, 114, 139; Thomas Daniel Young and George Core (eds.), *Selected Letters of John Crowe Ransom* (Baton Rouge, 1985), 239.

ence and literature are two different kinds of discourse and use different kinds of language; one is explicit and literal, the other implicit and evocative. To point up the differences between the order of knowledge provided by science and that available in literature, Ransom reiterates a point he had made more than ten years before: It would seem that science comes first with its highly selective rendering of a given reality, which consists in attending to some single one of its aspects; art comes afterwards, in what mood we may imagine, and attempts to restore the body which science has emptied.[5]

In *The New Criticism* (1941), Ransom examines in detail and from a single point of view the critical principles of some of the most important critics of his time. He assesses the value of each critic's contribution by measuring it against his theory of the ontological critic, which had been evolving for many years but was fully developed for the first time in the last essay in the book. He approves of I. A. Richards' close attention to the concrete particularities of the poem, but he castigates him for not accepting the cognitive function of poetry. William Empson, who "went to school" to Richards, is referred to as "the closest and most resourceful reader that poetry has ever had" because he reacts perceptively and sensitively to the textural details of a poem. His most obvious weakness is his inclination to lose sight of the poem's basic argument. Although T. S. Eliot possesses a "critical sense which is expert and infallible," he is deficient in critical theory, and like Richards, he argues that poetry's main function is to release emotion, thus de-emphasizing its cognitive function. Ransom approves of Yvor Winters' assertion that good poetry commands its reader's belief but feels that Winters fails to differentiate between the rational content of a poem and that of a prose discourse. Since none of these critics emphasizes sufficiently the essential duality of poetry, a point that Ransom has insisted upon for more than twenty years, he again attempts to identify poetic discourse by commenting on its odd structure, one which is not as "tight and precise on its logical side as a scientific prose structure generally is" but one which "imparts and carries along a great deal of irrelevant or foreign matter which is

5. Young and Core (eds.), *Selected Letters of John Crowe Ransom*, 256, 279–80, 156.

clearly not structural but even obstructive." Thus, he concludes, a poem must be regarded as having both a "loose logical structure" and an "irrelevant local texture." One way to identify the cognitive function of poetry is to examine the way in which the poem differs from logical discourse:

> The structure proper is the prose of the poem, being a logical discourse of almost any kind, and dealing with almost any suitable content. The texture, likewise, seems to be of any real content that may be come upon, provided it is so free, unrestricted, and extended that it cannot properly get into the structure. One guesses that it is an *order* of content rather than a kind of content that distinguishes texture from structure, and poetry from prose. At any rate, a moral content is a kind of content which has been suggested as the peculiar content of poetry, and it does not work; it is not really peculiar to poetry but perfectly available for prose. I suggest that the differentia of poetry as discourse is an ontological one. It treats an order of existence, a grade of objectivity, which cannot be treated in scientific discourse.
>
> This should not prove unintelligible. We live in a world that must be distinguished from the world, or the worlds, for there are many of them, which we treat in our scientific discourses. They are its reduced, emasculated and docile versions. Poetry intends to recover the denser and more refractory original world which we know loosely through our perceptions and memories. By this supposition it is a kind of knowledge which is radically or ontologically distinct.[6]

None of the literary critics whose work he has examined, Ransom concludes, has "an ontological account" of poetry. The nearest anyone he has read has come to developing such a conception of poetry is Charles W. Morris, whose most important works, as far as this discussion is concerned, are "Science, Art and Technology" and "Aesthetics and the Theory of Signs," two essays in which he applies to art the semantic system developed in *Foundations of the Theory of Signs*. Although Morris comes close—

---

6. John Crowe Ransom, "I. A. Richards, the Psychological Critic, and William Empson, His Pupil," in Ransom, *The New Criticism* (Norfolk, Conn., 1941), 102; Ransom, "T. S. Eliot: The Historical Critic," *ibid.*, 146; Ransom, "Yvor Winters: The Logical Critic," *ibid.*, 211–75; Ransom, "Wanted: An Ontological Critic," *ibid.*, reprinted in Thomas Daniel Young and John Hindle (eds.), *Selected Essays of John Crowe Ransom* (Baton Rouge, 1984), 147–48.

only one step more would have "taken him to an ontological conception of poetry"—he does not go far enough to satisfy Ransom. Morris distinguishes three forms of discourse—science, art, and technology—and he identifies three dimensions of meaning: the semantical, the syntactical, and the pragmatical. This kind of distinction suggests the basic difference between art and science first recognized by the ancient Greeks: "Art, like technology, is concerned with making something as well as knowing something"; while pure science seems concerned only with knowing something. What poetry makes is the poem, which because it contains meter is a "manufactured form," a "special unit of discourse." Like science, Morris argues, art provides knowledge, but the knowledge produced by science differs from that available in art because science employs "symbols," which merely refer to other objects, but art uses "icons" or images, which not only *refer* to other objects but *resemble* those objects. Thus the object symbolized by the scientific sign is abstract, a single property or aspect of an object; whereas the object symbolized by the aesthetic sign is the whole object. The scientific symbol refers to "man," but the aesthetic sign represents "this particular man." The aesthetic sign, as Ransom has been insisting for years, restores to an abstract item the "body from which it was taken."[7]

With Morris' distinction between the aesthetic and the scientific sign, Ransom is, of course, in complete agreement. But why, he asks, is Morris content to stop with the rather vague statement that the "icon embodies some . . . value-property"? Why does he not proceed to the logical assertion that aesthetic discourse has a useful pragmatic function? To indicate how he thinks his questions should be answered, Ransom moves to his ontological argument by rephrasing the distinction between scientific and aesthetic discourse he had insisted on since the middle twenties. Since the validity of scientific discourse depends upon its "semantical purity," it employs symbols which refer to an object specifically defined and its reference is always limited and uniform. The icon of aesthetic discourse, on the other hand, refers always to the wholeness of an object and embodies the value property of the object represented; therefore it can be neither

7. Young and Hindle (eds.), *Selected Essays of John Crowe Ransom*, 148–50.

limited nor defined. The icon does not function with the logical exactness of the scientific symbol because it often digresses at many points from its "logical pattern." For this reason the full meaning of a poem is never included in its prose paraphrase. The world with which scientific discourse deals is always predictable, limited, and restrictive. The world of art cannot be restricted, and the icon used to represent it always attempts to give a sense of the actual objects. Ransom thus reiterates the central point of "The Third Moment," the unpublished essay on which he worked intermittently between 1926 and 1930. Poetry intends not to issue some comment upon an experience but to reconstitute the experience itself. Scientific knowledge and aesthetic knowledge are not intended to replace each other. They are really alternate knowledges, which should illuminate and complement each other. Science can never produce for us a world made of "whole and indefeasible objects," but poetry can and does. The loose and imprecise poetic structure with its "irrelevant or foreign matter" is a means of acquiring an order of knowledge that we cannot know otherwise.[8]

Almost as soon as *The New Criticism* was published, Ransom wrote Tate of his dissatisfaction with the book. He saw immediately that he had "sacrificed the critics" in order to get his "own oar in." The book's chief fault, he wrote on January 5, 1942, is its lack of focus, its divided purpose. He had attempted to summarize the critical principles of four major critics and at the same time to develop his own theory of the nature and function of poetry. His sense of failure was so acute that he proposed to undertake immediately a new book in which he could develop in more detail his theory of aesthetics. He wished particularly to be able to pursue further his views of the nature of poetic discourse in order to indicate the specific qualities of structure and texture and to demonstrate the significance of their complex relationships in a poem. He was convinced, too, that the book failed to achieve another, and equally meaningful, objective. He had hoped to free from suspicion and "philosophical censorship" those critics who were doing the formal, analytical criticism essential to the delineation of the unique nature of the poetic dis-

---

8. *Ibid.*, 153; Ransom, *The World's Body*, x.

course, those who were intent upon restoring poetry to a place of central importance in a society no longer aware of its significance.[9] The book proposed here was never written, but during the next few years Ransom published a series of articles devoted almost entirely to the single purpose of demonstrating how the critic can justify the existence of poetry in a society more and more dependent upon the quasi knowledge of science. In the mid-1940s, Ransom warned some of his fellow critics, who he thought should take some new directions, that the "ingenious and sophisticated" literary masterpieces produced in the years immediately following World War I have been defined and mastered and are now available to the entire literary community. Although one need has been met, others remain. If literature is to be an important force in human affairs, the critics must continue their evaluations of older literatures in the light of modern standards, and they must intensify their studies of the "structural techniques of fiction" and "the diction and tropology of poetry." They must assist the reader in understanding the human purpose that drives the literary critic into the literary world of fantasy and imagination. To accomplish this purpose, whatever the particular area of their concern, they must help the reader perceive the reality of literary form, to become aware of its unique nature, of how a poem or story functions. Ransom insists that no reader can derive from a poem all the meanings it embodies unless he is aware of the unique nature of the poetic structure. In their proper emphasis on the total connotation of words, some commentators have failed to recognize sufficiently other essential aspects of the poem:

> The detailed phrase is honored with the spread of its own meaning, though this meaning may be away from that of the poem as a whole. And the critic goes straight from one detail to another, in the manner of the bee who gathers honey from the several blossoms as he comes to them, without noticing the bush which supports all the blossoms. The poem is more generous than the bush in its capacity for bearing blossoms which are not alike but widely varied in size, fragrance, hue, and shape.

9. John Crowe Ransom to Allen Tate, January 5, 1942, in Jesse E. Wills Fugitive/Agrarian Collection, Special Collections, Jean and Alexander Heard Library, Vanderbilt University.

Although many of the modern critics make the reader aware of the "exciting turns of poetic language," some of them do not reveal the poem's true nature because they are "careless of the theoretical constitution of poetry." They reveal the textural richness of the poem but neglect its basic structure.[10]

During the last decade of his editorship of the *Kenyon Review*, Ransom produced some of his most important critical writing, essays which show his continued preoccupation with the unique structure of poetic discourse and demonstrate the remarkable consistency of his critical position over a period of fifty years. In many of these essays, he covers much of the ground he has been over before as he tries to clear up misunderstood statements or badly expressed concepts. His definition of a poem, however, is unchanged, even in language; a poem remains a "logical structure having a local texture." In "Old Age of an Eagle," he indicates his unhappiness with this twofold division of the poem by presenting its three dimensions: "First the plot, or argument, a human representation struck off smartly, developed clearly and rounded off to a nicety. Then the meters . . . and finally, the poetic language, the flowering habit of a thing that is alive, displaying its grace generally and coming into intermittent focus in special configurations of leaf or blossoms." Despite the differences in terminology and the obvious intention to give more emphasis to meter, this statement adds little to his assertion that a poem has two kinds of meanings: the "ostensible argument" (the structure), which may be reduced to prose, and the "tissue of meaning" (texture), which may not. Again he insists that though a poem is not "included in its paraphrase," it must "include its own paraphrase." In spite of the protests of some critics that this structure-texture formulation is too near the false division of the poem into form and content, Ransom reiterates his conviction that the poetic discourse has a logical structure which can be rendered in a prose paraphrase. Such an exercise is "useful" and "reputable," he argues, because it "straightens out the text and prunes meaning down," so that the critic can demonstrate that the poem is "decent enough to make formal sense." Almost with-

---

10. John Crowe Ransom, "Poetry: The Formal Analysis," *Kenyon Review*, IX (Summer, 1947), 436.

out explanation, though he will return to this point in a later essay, he divides his "structure" into "plot" and "meter," but with the exception of meter, "plot" retains all the characteristics formerly lodged in "structure," and "poetic language" replaces "texture." He suggests that the structure-texture dualism may be explained in terms of Freud's discussion of the ego and the id. The "thought work" in a poem, its structure, belongs to the ego, but the "interpolated material which does not relate to the argument" is the work of the id. "A powerful sensibility is recording in the poem," he reminds his reader, "and the result might be a tropical wilderness of dense figurations, therefore humanly a waste, a nothing; but an equally powerful scheme of order is working there, too, to manage the riches of sense." A poem may be regarded, therefore, as a creation conceived under both sensibility and intelligence acting in "opposed parts," like counterpoint in music.[11]

Two of Ransom's most significant essays are those which he published in the mid-1950s on the Concrete Universal. Although less an essay than a series of partially developed reflections on the subject, the first of these begins with W. K. Wimsatt's statement that a "poem is a structure which may be viewed as a Concrete Universal." This definition of poetic discourse Ransom finds only partially acceptable, as he does Hegel's understanding of poetry. Ransom agrees, he says, with Hegel's argument that the "author of the poem is Spirit residing . . . in the poet and identical with that Spirit of the Universe which is God or that Spirit of History which continually creates in order to objectify itself." The amplitude of this Spirit, therefore, is so great that it can be expressed only through the "plenitude of concreteness" and not through abstract scientific concepts. He cannot accept, however, Hegel's argument that poetic language is "perfect Synthesis of the Thesis (or Universal) and the Antithesis (or Concrete)," that the Concrete is wholly assimilated in the Universal. The logical argument of a poem never incorporates within itself all the irrelevant textural details; therefore, the Universal never

11. John Crowe Ransom, "Old Age of an Eagle," in Ransom, *Poems and Essays* (New York, 1955), 79–87; Ransom, "More Than Gesture," *Partisan Review,* XX (January–February, 1953), 111.

quite grasps the Concrete, and the prose paraphrase is never equivalent to the poem.[12]

This discussion of the Concrete Universal leads him not only to reassert his belief in the significance of poetry in a world almost completely dominated by science but also to attempt again to define the unique nature of the poem, this time by describing how language functions in its development:

> About fifteen years ago I was thinking of the poem as having a logical structure or framework, and a texture whose character was partly irrelevant to the logical form and purpose. My "texture" in particular has given offense, and the fact is that I had no sooner uttered it than it struck me as a flat and inadequate figure for that vivid and easily felt part of the poem which we associate peculiarly with poetic language. I wish now to recast my definition entirely, though I shall only employ another figure whose disabilities I am aware of in advance. . . . Suppose we say that the poem is an organism. Then it has a physiology. We will figure its organs, and to me it seems satisfactory if we say there are three: the head, the heart, the feet. In this organism the organs work all at the same time, but the peculiarity of the joint production is that it still consists of the products of the organs working individually.

All of these organs work together to produce a poem, but each retains its individual character. Each speaks out in a different language: "the head in an intellectual language, the heart in an affective language, the feet in a rhythmical language." On the intellectual level, the poem is a logical whole, with a beginning, a middle, and an end; it also contains whatever connective devices are needed to suggest relationships among these various parts. But in addition to this intellectual level, which he had formerly referred to as the structure, the poem has a cluster of rich particulars which evoke a variety of responses in its readers. Many modern critics focus so much of their attention upon the richness of the particulars, upon the individual phrase and the specific figure, that they leave the impression that a poem cannot be perceived of as a complete whole. It can be, but only if one remains constantly aware of the unique nature of the poetic discourse.

---

12. John Crowe Ransom, "The Concrete Universal: Observations on the Understanding of Poetry, I," *Kenyon Review*, XVI (Autumn, 1954), 554–64.

Although the three organs of a poem—the head, the heart, and the feet—speak different languages and retain their individual voices, they blend to form one sound. They work together to produce one poem, but the unity of a poem is as that of a "democratic government" not that of a "totalitarian state." A poem, he says in another essay, is like a house with the paint, paper, and tapestry comparable to the texture and the roof and beams to the structure. He does not concede for the poem a view of totality that would make it operate as a machine does, for to allow this concession would force him to admit that a poem is a scientific Universal in which the Concrete particular is assimilated in the abstract Universal. Instead he insists that the essential unity of a poem exists in interrelationships of its individual parts.[13]

This statement is the germ of Ransom's argument in his second essay on the Concrete Universal, in which he demonstrates why he regards Kant, and not Hegel, as his mentor. A Universal, as Hegel used the term, is "any idea in the mind which proposes a little universe, or organized working combination of parts," in order to attempt to produce a single effect. The Universal, which is an idea, a design as it exists in the understanding, creates this single impression only when each part performs its several duties, and it becomes a Concrete Universal when it is actually working. A chemical formula, a recipe, a blueprint, or even Newman's idea of a university may be considered examples of Universals. There are two kinds of Concrete Universals: 1) those of applied science in which there is "not one necessary part missing; nor one unnecessary part showing," each part acting precisely as it should; 2) and those of the arts, of poetry, which do not satisfy an organic need and are not located in the "animal perspective of human nature."[14]

From Kant's view of the Concrete Universal, Ransom has learned, he continues, to distinguish between the different kinds

---

13. *Ibid.*, 559; John Crowe Ransom, "Criticism as Pure Speculation," in Donald A. Stauffer (ed.), *The Intent of the Critic* (Princeton, 1941), 91–124.

14. John Crowe Ransom, "The Concrete Universal: Observations on the Understanding of Poetry, II," in Young and Hindle (eds.), *Selected Essays of John Crowe Ransom*, 289–90.

of Universals: the scientific Universal has a practical end in mind and will not hesitate to alter the materials of nature until they fit a preconceived concept. The critic accepting this view of the Concrete Universal would insist that the "Concrete is used up so completely in the service of Universal that there is no remainder." The Concrete particulars of the poem are completely integrated into the abstract Universal. Poetry, however, is a moral Universal and differs radically from the scientific Universal: "The moral Universal of the poem does not use nature as a means but as an end; it goes out into nature not as a predatory conquerer and despoiler but as an inquirer, to look at nature as nature naturally is and see what its own reception there may be." The moral Universal does not go to nature, as the scientific Universal does, to "ransack for materials which . . . [have already been] exacted." For this reason the critic should not expect the "unpredictable and highly particular detail" of the region of nature used in the poem to "enter precisely and without remainder into the formal Universal." The pure Universal, being a concept in the mind, will not stand confrontation with the actual world and will always appear fragmentary and distorted in the light of the world's unpredicated and phenomenal mystery. The complete realization of this pure Universal, only a portion of which is included in the scientific Universal, is the Concrete Universal. This Concrete Universal may be found in poetry of the right kind: not didactic verse, which tells us how to act, nor in that verse which attempts to prescribe a specific mode of thought, but in the poetry which assists the reader in knowing the world. In poetry of this type, the imagination, through metaphor, makes the pure Universal, which is abstract and conceptual, perceptual and Concrete: The Universal is referred to nature and particularized, given sensuous detail through this reference. Nature is, therefore, an essential element for poetry, but the organization of a poem does not require that the logical plan of the poem be "borne out perfectly in the sensuous detail which puts it into action."[15]

Ransom's lack of sympathy for the rational monism of Hegel and his followers did not diminish as the years passed, and his last published essay was entitled "The Concrete Universal." In

15. *Ibid.*, 291, 290.

1970, when this essay was published, he was still intrigued by the implications of a phrase "in which two terms radically opposed must continue leaning upon each other till they fall hopelessly apart." The phrase suggests a union of the individual or particular and the abstract, and Ransom still insists that it cannot be made to work "naturally and meaningfully." Because it is "hopelessly abstract" and "composed of mere concepts," the scientific Universal can only hope to keep what it "wants of the World" and to reject more than it takes. The scientific Universal cannot hope to represent completely those occasions "when the world somewhere seems possessed and sustained through and through by the concretions of the spirit," when a "natural landscape is utterly beautiful, with every feature adapted to the common tone," when "there is realized beside some hearth a scene of perfect familial accord," or when " a whole people is exalted in a moment of crisis by the consciousness of serving a just state." Simply defined, Ransom concludes, a poem is "an organism in action," and he again labels its organs the head, the heart, and the feet. Although each organ plays its separate part, it must reconcile its differences with the other two in order to form a harmonious whole. The three organs "are harmonizing and vocalizing all at the same time," but, he insists, the poem is both a "verbal and vocal job"; therefore this vocalism is not "like the outpourings of operatic or instrumental music." The function of each organ is distinct and always identifiable, even in a finished poem:

> The head has to be the intellectual organ, and especially attentive to keeping the logical clarity of the text, and the finality of the conclusion. It has as much conscience in this respect as prose has, and is slow to waive its simple purity; for instance if the heart tries its patience by wanting to use words and phrases which are fateful and strange but too rich and rare for the common barbarian reader. But just often enough it is possible to persuade the honest head that a quotidian language will not do for good verse; till the head finally concurs, and is rewarded by receiving some rare intimations of immortality.

But this exchange between the head and the heart is always imperfect; furthermore the feet—the meters, rhymes, and rhythms—always make their demands and often at the expense of the head and the heart. Thus the Concrete particulars are never completely consumed in an abstract Universal.[16]

To the end of his life, therefore, Ransom continued to argue for the essential duality of poetry. He differs most obviously from the positivists, who in their attempts to show that poetry makes positive sense, accept the prose argument of the poem as its center and contend that the multiplicity of suggestions in the metaphor form another argument which is also true and useful. To accept this position, Ransom insists, is to "convert poetry into prose, and to contend that its radical departures from prose are only illusory." Although he continues to argue that poetic texture is "poetic and, irremediably, not positive," he also insists that this texture attaches itself "technically to a positive center," which it does not destroy. The latter part of this argument has not been well received by other critics, particularly Cleanth Brooks, who is convinced that the kind of duality Ransom defends is too near the age-old dichotomy of form and content and can lead to the erroneous conclusion that a poem consists of a "prose sense decorated by a sensuous imagery." To Brooks, structure is a "structure of meanings, evaluations, and interpretations" and its unity consists of "balancing and harmonizing connotations, attitudes and meanings." This attitude, Ransom reasons, denies the poem any formal shape except that which might evolve from the unfolding of its metaphorical energy. Such a definition does not embrace "that character in the poem which makes it discourse." He repeats his assertion that a poem is a "species of Aristotelian discourse," with a beginning, middle, and end, "if the argument is sizable enough to worry about such things."[17]

For Ransom the poem remains "the great paradox, a construct looking two ways, with logic trying to dominate the metaphors and metaphors trying to dominate the logic." To this contrary twosome he adds meter to give the poem "the form of a trinitarian existence" and to make its creation dependent upon a tenuous compromise between meter and sense, image and idea, metaphor and argument. From this combination of heteroge-

16. John Crowe Ransom, "The Concrete Universal," in Ransom, *Beating the Bushes* (New York, 1972), 176.
17. John Crowe Ransom, "Positivists and Near Positive Aesthetics," *ibid.*, 73.

neous qualities comes almost the only defense man has against the encroachments of science and technology, for poetry is one of the few means through which man can reconstitute the qualitative particularity of experience. It assists man in recalling the "body and solid substance of the world" from the "fulness of memory" to which it has retired.[18]

(1976)

18. Ransom, *The World's Body*, x.

A Little Divergence: The Critical Theories of John Crowe Ransom and Cleanth Brooks

WHEN Cleanth Brooks came from his home in west Tennessee to enter the freshman class of Vanderbilt University, John Crowe Ransom was awaiting reaction to *Chills and Fever*, his second volume of verse. Since his return from service in France in World War I, Ransom had offered regularly his courses in advanced composition and modern literature, courses that had enrolled, among others, Merrill Moore, Andrew Lytle, Allen Tate, and Robert Penn Warren. Then in its third year and to live one more before its demise in December, 1925, the *Fugitive*, to which Ransom had contributed most of his mature poetry, was already proclaimed "one of the best journals of its kind available." Although the administration of Vanderbilt University had not formally recognized the existence of the group of faculty members and students who were participating in one of the most significant literary ventures of this century, students of Brooks's cast were well aware of what was transpiring in those Saturday evening meetings in the home of James M. Frank. One of Brooks's sensibility surely found the atmosphere on the campus exhilarating. In the corridors of College Hall he passed every day men who not only were writing poetry but were publishing their verse, his first association with poets outside the pages of a textbook. But, as he wrote many years later, "My Vanderbilt years were—as far as having John's tutelage was concerned—largely wasted. A melancholy reflection. I have only myself, in my ignorance and innocence, and my confused romanticism, to blame."

This essay originally appeared, in slightly different form, in *The Possibilities of Order: Cleanth Brooks and His Work*, ed. Lewis P. Simpson (Baton Rouge, 1976). Reprinted by permission of the Louisiana State University Press.

Because he was "too much in awe" of the man who had already received national notice as poet and man of letters and because he felt he "was not ready for the work the class was doing," Brooks dropped Ransom's course in modern literature, in which he had enrolled at the beginning of his sophomore year. Although he never acted on his resolution to take the course before he graduated, he did complete during his junior year the advanced composition. But Ransom's earliest influence on Brooks, unlike that on Donald Davidson, Tate, and Warren, was not in the classroom but through his poetry. "I couldn't make much of his poetry," Brooks wrote in February, 1973, "until my senior year. Then, one evening, idly looking at one of his volumes lying on a table before me, I started reading the poems and something happened. I found them fascinating and wondered how I had missed their quality before. This is not to say that I suddenly understood every word and phrase. But their general import was clear and their stylistic brilliance hit me hard." What Ransom had done for the brilliant and sensitive young student was to take "literature off the library shelf, blow the dust off," and convince him that it "is alive and wonderfully important." This conviction undoubtedly assisted Brooks in determining his formal vocation.

In September, 1928, after his graduation from Vanderbilt the previous June, Brooks enrolled in Tulane University, from which he earned the master of arts degree the following June. While he was in New Orleans, he "began to see Ransom's poetry for what it was"; he began to "read him hard and continued to do so in the years that followed." From Oxford, where he studied as a Rhodes scholar from 1929 to 1932, he wrote Donald Davidson that he had just read *God Without Thunder* and that Ransom's statement of the place and function of religion in twentieth-century society was the most plausible and convincing treatment of that subject he had seen. "I was frankly surprised at Ransom's position," he wrote, "and delighted—partially perhaps because his book represents a more mature and sensitive statement of the position I had been working toward; e.g. I found the same significance in C. C. Ayres' *Science: A False Messiah*. I had the same interpretation of Kant and Hume. I had found the same hostility and withering skepticism in the anthropologists. . . . I am at this time writing Ransom a long letter telling him what I think of his book."

This letter was followed by others, and during the winter and spring of 1931 to 1932, Brooks visited Ransom in Devonshire, where he and his family were living while he was studying on a Guggenheim grant. After receiving a B.Litt. degree from Oxford in the spring of 1932, Brooks accepted a position at Louisiana State University, where two years later he was joined by Robert Penn Warren. In 1935, the first issue of the *Southern Review* appeared, with Brooks and Warren as managing editors, and during the next few years that distinguished journal carried more of Ransom's essays than any other publication. Although any contribution from Ransom was cordially received in Baton Rouge, its acceptance for publication was not always assured, as indicated by the reception of Ransom's controversial "Shakespeare at Sonnets."

On October 18, 1937, Ransom wrote Brooks: "I enclose the 'Shakespeare at Sonnets' about which I spoke to you at Allen's last summer. It is the last piece I have felt it necessary to do for completion of my MS [*The World's Body*], which I have delayed sending in till this one was off. . . . I note that I am being a little rough on Shakespeare in a magazine edited by two great Shakespeareans." The response by the "two great Shakespeareans" to the essay is apparently lost, but its general tone is suggested in a letter Ransom wrote Allen Tate on November 4:

> The boys deal pretty pedantically with my poor paper, you will see. . . . I wrote them a pretty warm letter but after thinking it over withheld it and wrote another. I also revised the thing, adding a bit, taking account of points of theirs which seemed to me worth anything, generally improving it. . . . I really stepped on their toes a little, come to think about it. For Red is a Shakespearean, and would not like my irresponsible knocks for the comfort of the Philistines; and Cleanth is an expert on metaphysical poetry, and thinks everybody ought to discuss the thing in his minute terms. They are a bit magisterial, or is it just my own oversensitive imagination?

Whatever the objections, they must have been satisfied by Ransom's revisions, for he wrote Tate on November 19: "A nice note from the boys at Baton Rouge says they're printing my piece. I suppose they felt aggrieved at my high tone, but they don't extend the argument further." The essay was published in the winter issue, 1938.[1]

---

1. Thomas Daniel Young and George Core (eds.), *Selected Letters of John Crowe Ransom* (Baton Rouge, 1985), 233.

A few months later, Brooks sent Ransom the proof sheets of *Modern Poetry and the Tradition*, most of the essays in which Ransom had not read, and asked for the "honest reaction I always get from you." From Austin, where he was serving as visiting professor for the summer, Ransom responded immediately. "The book stands up," he wrote. "The most unified of all the fine critical books of our day, with [the] possible exception of Empson, coming to a fine climax with the chapter on reform of literary history." That Ransom could not accept some of its major conclusions, however, is indicated in the paragraph following the previously quoted sentence:

> Your position is argued with patient and persuasive logic & illustration. It's an extreme position, as I think, and held with extreme almost dogmatic tenacity. You never discuss any *limit* to complication, and you tend to think that *any* complication in a modern is logical or functional complication, whereas poor Burns' *my luve's like a red, red rose* is not functional or logical. To most readers it will seem that *Waste Land* is excessive complication and no unit poem at all, after reading your exposition.
>
> You do a similar disservice to Yeats. You put into the 17th C[entury] tradition poems that no 17th C[entury] poet would have approved. You use *wit* too broadly, or else you do wrong to the poetry in requiring it; and irony. *Lycidas* and Virgil and all Great poetry falls by your estimates....
>
> Yet I believe this is about the ablest book that's appeared. Its error if any is on the side of the angels.[2]

As soon as the book was published, a copy came to the office of the *Kenyon Review*, and Ransom wrote Brooks apologizing for not being able to review it immediately. Since he already had a twelve-page essay in the current number, he was extremely reluctant to "appear on more pages than that of my own journal." But in the next issue he planned to "editorialize, and give it the very best send-off, with a haggling reservation or two towards the end to make the review decently 'objective.'" This "haggling reservation or two" is anticipated in the comments with which he closed the paragraph referring to the book: "As I have pondered on your general position I am most doubtful about your references to science. I have the idea that any definite and positive structural pattern discoverable in the poem, or anywhere on earth for that matter, is an act of science, not a peculiar act of

2. *Ibid.*, 247.

poetry; unless you want poetry to rate merely as superior science. Science is not simple as you imply. . . . You . . . seem to be primarily interested in displaying functional structure. For me, at the present, that's not quite the main cue."[3]

The association between the two men became closer during the late thirties and early forties. In addition to the frequent exchange of letters and manuscripts, which always included requests for reaction and comment, there was considerable discussion of joint editorial ventures of the two journals. Some of their most ambitious plans were interrupted, however, by the coming of World War II and its effect on the national economy. Ransom wrote Tate on January 5, 1942, that Warren had warned him of the demise of the *Southern Review* and, on January 28, that there was a strong possibility that the *Kenyon Review* would have to be discontinued. The faculty committee appointed by the president of the college to study the budget might decide, he feared, that the *Review* was a luxury rather than "an 'educational necessity.'" Whatever that committee's decision, he was faced with the immediate prospect of having to decrease by one-half the honoraria to contributors, of having to employ a student-secretary, and of being able to publish only three times a year. "But here's a possibility," he concluded. "Upon the announced demise of the Southern Review I wrote the boys to please come in and 'merge' with the Kenyon Review." If such an arrangement could be worked out, he intended to use the cover of the *Southern Review* and print on it the names of both journals. He would publish all of their accepted contributions, honor their unexpired subscriptions, and list on the title page all three names as editors. "We'd make this joint editorship real in every workable sense," he wrote, "and we could easily by arranging some sort of exchange have one of them up here a part of each year, on the faculty, and on the grounds."[4]

While the necessarily involved negotiations were continuing at Baton Rouge and between Brooks and Warren there and Ransom in Gambier, the financial condition of the *Kenyon Review* considerably worsened. Ransom was convinced that he could not continue publication beyond 1942 unless he could discover a generous outside donor; nevertheless, he prepared a

3. *Ibid.*, 262.
4. *Ibid.*, 289.

budget anticipating the merger of the two journals, and he wrote Tate in early February outlining in minute detail his plans for the combined publication. As late as May 22, no decision had been reached concerning the proposed merger, though Brooks and Warren had announced the previous fall that their journal faced "suspension of publication with the spring issue of 1942." At this time there appeared the statement, "The Editors regret that with the present number the *Southern Review* ceases publication" but that "unexpired subscriptions will be filled by the *Kenyon Review*." Although a complete merger of the two journals was never effected, the *Kenyon Review* was paid $750 to fill the unexpired subscriptions of the *Southern*, and the masthead of the *Kenyon*, beginning with the autumn issue, carried as advisory editors the names of both Brooks and Warren.[5]

That Brooks took his appointment seriously is indicated by the steady flow of reviews and articles he submitted and by his detailed and generous comments on the prospective contributions on which Ransom asked his opinion. While serving as advisory editor, he contributed more than a dozen articles and reviews to the *Kenyon Review*. During the fall and winter of 1943 to 1944, he spent a considerable amount of time arranging for a symposium on the poetry of Gerard Manley Hopkins, which included contributions by Austin Warren, Josephine Miles, Marshall McLuhan, and Harold Whitehall and which was published in the autumn issue, 1944. From the inauguration of the Kenyon School of English in 1948 and for the three years of its existence, Brooks served as one of its Fellows, and for its first session he joined a distinguished faculty, including Eric Bentley, Richard Chase, F. O. Matthiessen, William Empson, Austin Warren, Allen Tate, and Ransom. Each member of the faculty taught one course and made at least one appearance before the entire student body. Brooks offered a course in Milton and gave as his public lecture a discussion of Milton's metaphors. As soon as possible after his return to Yale, he wrote Ransom his impressions of that innovative educational experience. "I should have written earlier," he began, "to tell you what I have told others, that the first session of the K[enyon] S[chool] seemed to me a brilliant success. The students to whom I talked, particularly the more mature students and auditors, were unanimous in saying

5. *Ibid.*, 290–92, 296.

this. Actually none of us who were personally involved can be the most impartial judges; even so, having made this discount, I think all of us have a right to think the school was brilliantly launched."

Over a period of forty years or more, Ransom and Brooks were close friends. Although they were never able to spend a great deal of time together, they often lamented this fact, and their letters contain repeated references to needing and desiring the opportunity for long discussions of literary and personal matters. Whenever busy schedules would permit, visits were arranged, even at the expense of further complicating travel arrangements already uncomfortably involved. At the same time, each followed closely the development of the other's professional career. Ransom wrote extensive and masterful reviews of Brooks's books as they appeared; Brooks, in turn, produced some of the most helpful commentary yet available on Ransom. In addition to the sections devoted to him in both *Modern Poetry and the Tradition* and *The Well Wrought Urn,* Brooks analyzes and evaluates Ransom's theories and practices, both as poet and critic, in some of the most informative and convincing of his essays.

In spite of the mutual affection and respect these two men shared for more than four decades, they did not always agree on literary theory. In both we have the insistence that literature embodies the highest values of the culture from which it comes and that these values cannot be transmitted to its consumers—to the readers of poetry, for example—unless the art object is given the closest scrutiny possible. The manner in which this examination should occur was always of first importance to Ransom and remains a major concern for Brooks. When Ransom once wrote that he and Brooks were about "as like as two peas from the same pod," he was referring to personal similarities. Both grew up in small Tennessee towns, the sons of Methodist ministers; both were educated at Vanderbilt and Oxford. In spite of these similarities "we have diverged a little," Ransom wrote; and though he was concerned about some of Brooks's "departures," it was always with the feeling that he was contending with his alter ego. For, he concluded, if "Brooks and I were being landed on the desert island, I have no doubt that the books we would severally take along would be the same books, and chosen in the same order, and we would read them in unison."[6] Here, it would seem, Ransom was suggesting the nature of their critical disagreement. Both agreed on the function of poetry. It assumes a necessary place in the life of the civilized man because it contains a unique kind of knowledge; he can learn from it that which he can get nowhere else. But this consensus of opinion regarding the uses of poetry did not carry over into their discussions of its basic nature. Ransom believed that Brooks had overstated his case in insisting that wit, paradox, and irony are essential elements of poetry; Brooks was not persuaded that Ransom's argument for logical structure in a poem does not destroy its essential unity by suggesting a split between form and content. A review of the published commentary on each other's work not only reveals these similarities and differences but also reminds us of the extent to which both Ransom and Brooks have influenced literary theory and practice during the past three or four decades....

Even at the time Ransom wrote ["Criticism, Inc."], he was undoubtedly aware that he was not alone in his request for a new approach to literary study, for criticism concerned with formal analysis and literary judgments, for specific examples of the kinds of insights one can obtain only from the study of the literary documents themselves. Since the inception of the *Southern Review,* Robert Penn Warren and Cleanth Brooks had been seeking for publication critical essays and reviews based upon the intensive and sensitive experiences with the works of art for which Ransom was calling; as a matter of fact, during the three years of the journal's existence more than a dozen of Ransom's own essays and reviews had appeared in its pages. In 1938, the year Ransom's *The World's Body,* which included "Criticism, Inc.," was published, Brooks and Warren issued *Understanding Poetry,* a textbook which carried into the classroom the critical approach that Ransom desired.

The "Letter to the Teacher," with which this popular textbook opens, leaves no doubt where its emphasis is placed. The editors agree with Ransom that one can get from poetry, properly read, insights into the nature of human existence that he

6. John Crowe Ransom, "Why Critics Don't Go Mad," in Ransom, *Beating the Bushes* (New York, 1972), 161, 169.

can get almost nowhere else, but if poetry is to provide this kind of illumination it must be read as poetry and not as history, biography, or moral philosophy. The temptation to which too many readers and teachers of poetry have succumbed in the past is that of substituting something else for the poem. The most common substitutes are "paraphrase of logical and narrative content," "study of biographical and historical materials," and "inspirational and didactic interpretation." Although all of these may be important to one degree or another in the study of a poem, they should always be regarded as means and not as ends. The accumulation of this kind of information should not be confused with the essential literary activity, that of reading the poem itself. To teach poetry adequately and properly, the editors insist, one's teaching methods must include the following principles: "(1) Emphasis should be kept on the poem as a poem; (2) the treatment should be concrete and inductive; and (3) a poem should always be treated as an organic system of relationships, and the poetic quality should never be understood as inhering in one or more factors taken in isolation."[7] In an anthology of several hundred poems—arranged in order of increasing difficulty and complemented by analyses of individual poems and discussions of such poetic techniques and topics as "metrics," "tone and attitude," "imagery," and "statement and idea"—the editors demonstrate how this approach to poetry should function. It is hardly an overstatement to say that this book and its two companion volumes, *Understanding Fiction* (1943) and *Understanding Drama* (1945), the latter done by Brooks and Robert B. Heilman, have revolutionized the way literature is taught in the classroom.

In 1939, Brooks published *Modern Poetry and the Tradition*, which he says is dedicated to helping the reader, whose "conception of poetry is . . . primarily defined . . . by the achievement of the Romantic poets," understand and appreciate the poetry of his own age. Convinced that his generation of readers was "witnessing . . . a critical revolution of the order of the Romantic Revolt," he proposes to show the relationship of modern to traditional poetry and to demonstrate that the poetry of W. B. Yeats,

---

7. Robert Penn Warren and Cleanth Brooks (eds.), *Understanding Poetry: An Anthology for College Students* (New York, 1938), xi, xv.

T. S. Eliot, and their contemporaries, though sometimes difficult and obscure, is not incomprehensible. Many modern readers, Brooks argues, have difficulty with contemporary verse because they are accustomed to reading poetry in which images are mere ornaments used for clarity, vividness, and beauty and are not prepared for poetry in which much of the imagery seems to "demean rather than adorn . . . darken rather than illuminate."[8] Two other concepts, which go at least as far back as Joseph Addison, have prevented contemporary verse from receiving a fair hearing: Certain words and objects are intrinsically poetic and the intellectual faculty is opposed to the emotional or poetic faculty.

To get the proper perspective on the intentions of the modern poet, the argument continues, one must look beyond the romantic and Victorian poets to the metaphysicals, the last group to make full use of the prosaic, the difficult, the daring, the fanciful, and even the unpoetic. This study of the metaphysicals is necessary because the significant relationship between this group and the moderns is their "common conception of the use of metaphor" as opposed to the neoclassical and romantic poets. Following Thomas Hobbes, the neoclassic poets looked upon the role of the poet as that of copyist; the modern poets, like the metaphysicals, think the proper role of the poet is that of maker. The play of intellect in a poem is not necessarily hostile to the presentation of a sincere emotional experience. Often the complex attitudes that a poem expresses combine both emotion and intellect. The proper basis for judging the quality of any figure is to determine how it functions either positively or negatively; it "may serve irony as well as ennoblement." The only appropriate question, then, is, how well does it function in its own context?[9]

In the metaphysical poem, metaphor is essential because it *is* the poem. "Metaphor is not to be considered," Brooks argues, "as the alternative of the poet, which he may elect to use or not, since he may state the matter directly and straightforwardly if he chooses." Metaphor is often the only means of expressing the complex attitude with which the poet is concerned. This line of

---

8. Cleanth Brooks, *Modern Poetry and the Tradition* (Chapel Hill, 1939), viii–ix, 4.

9. *Ibid.*, 11, 15.

thought leads Brooks to two of his best-known critical statements. One, metaphorical language is not decoration or ornament; it *is* the poem and to remove it is to destroy the poem. Two, for this reason no poem can be reduced to paraphrase.[10]

Two of poetry's worst enemies, Brooks believes, were Thomas Hobbes and Matthew Arnold. Hobbes insisted that poetry is essentially statement and that the poet should endeavor to express "high poetic truth"; therefore, he will use clear illustrations, "illustrations which dignify and heighten." He will neither indulge in fanciful playfulness nor give the reader any reason to misunderstand his meaning. Arnold would remove everything from a poem that would seem to contradict what the poet wishes to communicate. Such views result in two common fallacies. The first is the didactic heresy, which insists that the end of poetry is to "instruct and convert." Those who hold this view are simply misinformed about the kind of truth poetry gives. A poem is "not a more or less true statement in metrical garb, but an organization of experience." The second fallacy insists that the poet should present his view of the experience simply and directly—a false conception that forces the poet into sentimentality, the result of the poet's sacrificing the totality of his vision and adopting a particular interpretation.[11]

Like Ransom, Brooks favors metaphysical poetry, a poetry that does not oversimplify the poet's view by omitting opposing and discordant elements but includes such elements and attempts to resolve them into a larger unity. Irony may result from the bringing together of the opposing impulses, and wit, as Eliot had previously defined the term, is the "poet's ability to synthesize diverse materials." The limiting term *metaphysical* may be applied to that kind of poetry in which the "opposition of the impulses which are united is extreme." Therefore, the poet is a maker with almost absolute confidence in the power of the imagination to remake his world "by relating into an organic whole the amorphous and heterogeneous and contradictory." A year earlier in his "Poetry: A Note in Ontology," Ransom had expressed his inclination for metaphysical poetry, in which the poet asserts his unscientific and miraculous predications over either physical poetry, a poetry almost devoid of idea, or Platonic

---

10. *Ibid.*, 15–17.
11. *Ibid.*, 35–37.

poetry, which "discourse[s] in things, but on the understanding that they are translatable at every point into ideas."[12]

Brooks summarizes the neoclassical age in this manner:

> The weakening of metaphor, the development of a specifically "poetic" subject matter and diction. The emphasis on simplicity and clarity, the simplification of the poet's attitude, the segregation of the witty and the ironical from the serious, the stricter separation of the various genres—all these items testify to the monopoly of the scientific spirit. This process of clarification involved the *exclusion* of certain elements from poetry—the prosaic, the unrefined, and the obscure. The imagination was weakened from a "magic and synthetic" power to Hobbes's conception of it as the file-clerk of the memory.[13]

The romantic movement was a reaction against many of these assumptions and, specifically, attempted to liberate the imagination. But the revolution was not severe enough and was not able to free itself from the conception that the function of poetry is didacticism. The importance of the new revolution, led by I. A. Richards, Eliot, Ransom, and Tate, is that it is attempting a complete liberation of the imagination. The most obvious result of the present critical revolution is in the successful use of "prosaic or unpleasant materials," in the "union of the intellectual with the emotional," and in the ability of the modern poet to "rid himself of clichés, worn-out literary materials, and the other stereotypes of Victorianism." The serious and intelligent reader of poetry will not refuse to give modern verse the kind of attention it deserves just because the poet refuses to oversimplify the experience he is presenting. If the scope and breadth of the experience he is assimilating is complex, this kind of reader will know that the poetic representation of that experience will necessarily be complex and may be even esoteric and obscure. The remainder of this book comprises detailed analyses of poems by Eliot, Yeats, Robert Frost, W. H. Auden, Tate, Warren, Ransom, and others. These exegeses are the kind of criticism Ransom called for in "Criticism, Inc." They concentrate on the poem as poem, they are concrete and inductive, and they insist that the poem is an indivisible unit, an organic system of relationships. Of most importance is their demonstration that, properly read,

---

12. *Ibid.*, 42, 43; John Crowe Ransom, "Poetry: A Note in Ontology," in Ransom, *The World's Body* (New York, 1938), 122, 128–42.
13. Brooks, *Modern Poetry and the Tradition*, 52.

poetry presents, in Ransom's terms, the "kind of knowledge by which we must know what we have arranged that we shall not know otherwise."[14]

In his review of *Modern Poetry and the Tradition*, which appeared in the Spring, 1940, *Kenyon Review*, Ransom complimented the *Southern Review*, "the organ of the most powerful critical discussion in the language." Its editors have been particularly "sympathetic with modern experimental poetry," and the book under consideration defends this editorial interest to the "point of brilliancy." He pointed immediately to Brooks's greatest strength: He is, "very likely, the most expert living 'reader' or interpreter of difficult verse." One of the greatest contributions of the book is in the exposition of difficult or obscure passages of modern verse, the significance of which would likely go by a less sensitive and imaginative reader.

In spite of Ransom's genuine admiration for the book, however, some of its theoretical assumptions and the conclusions based on these assumptions troubled him. In the first place, "its dialectic skims rather lightly over some of the deep places." He could not agree with Brooks's argument that "our difficult modern poetry, with all its 'wit' and 'richness,' has returned to the 17th century." Modern poetry differs from that of the metaphysicals in at least two important respects: The moderns have not had the "patience to achieve firm metrical structure" and their poetry is "equally lacking in firmness of logical argument." The seventeenth-century poets were infinitely superior in logic to those of either the eighteenth or the nineteenth century, and logic, he believed, is "more organic to the imaginative effect than Mr. Brooks will admit." Although Brooks argues convincingly for the superiority of twentieth-century poetry—with its irony, wit, and inclusiveness—over that of the eighteenth or nineteenth century, Ransom could not accept Brooks's thesis that symbolist poetry is very much like that of the English metaphysicals. The symbols of the English religious poetry of the seventeenth century were public and conventional, whereas those of the symbolist poets, and Eliot's *The Waste Land* belongs in this category, are esoteric, eclectic, and unsystematic. "Mr. Brooks," he concluded, "probably is the most accomplished reader of symbolist poetry who has spread his interpretations upon the record; but

14. Ransom, *The World's Body*, x.

his critical faculty has not yet attacked its problem, nor perhaps yet even acknowledged it."

In *Modern Poetry and the Tradition,* Brooks comments upon poetic unity and the manner in which logic functions in a poem:

> The only unity which matters in poetry is an imaginative unity. Logical unity when it occurs in a poem is valued, not in itself, but only as an element which may be brought into the larger imaginative unity—that is, it is not valued in itself unless we value the poem as science or as exhortation to a practical purpose. Logic may be used as a powerful instrument by the poet, as for example by Donne, but the logical unity does not organize the poem . . . the logic, though brilliant, is bad logic if we are to judge the poem on its value as a logical exercise. The show of logic, it is true, is justified; but it is justified in imaginative terms—not in logical terms. The logic is used to dictate a particular tone. It is really employed as a kind of metaphor. Non-logical relationships are treated here as if they were logical.[15]

Ransom's reaction to this passage is predictable. "I cannot think that is a satisfactory disposition of the function of the logic," he wrote, "and I would particularly covet a fuller treatment by Mr. Brooks of the relation of imagination to logic. The logic is probably more organic to the imaginative effect than Mr. Brooks will admit." The degree of Ransom's dissatisfaction with Brooks's treatment of the function of logic in the poem is most obvious in "Wanted: An Ontological Critic," the essay in which is given the best summary of the critical principles he held at this time. Particularly important to this discussion are his comments on the "odd structure" of the poem:

> What is the value of a structure which (a) is not so tight and precise on its logical side as a scientific or technical prose structure generally is, and (b) imports and carries along a great deal of irrelevant or foreign matter which is clearly not structural but even obstructive? . . . We sum it up by saying that the poem is a loose logical structure with an irrelevant logical texture.
> . . . The structure proper is the prose of the poem, being a logical discourse of almost any kind, and dealing with almost any content suited to a logical discourse.[16]

Ransom develops his argument by pointing out that the structure of a poem includes not only rhyme and meter but its logical

15. Brooks, *Modern Poetry and the Tradition,* 66–67.
16. John Crowe Ransom, "Wanted: An Ontological Critic," in Ransom, *The New Criticism* (Norfolk, Conn., 1941), 210.

content; the "illogical texture" is composed of diction, imagery, sound, and other "irrelevant" elements of art.

Brooks's reaction to Ransom's "texture-structure formulation" is most clearly expressed in "The Heresy of Paraphrase," a chapter in *The Well Wrought Urn* (1947). The structure of poetry, he states emphatically, is dramatic: A poem, like a play, arrives at its conclusion through conflict, and its resolution, which is also dramatic, is reached through analogical rather than logical means. The essential structure of a poem is a "pattern of resolved stresses . . . a pattern of resolutions and balances and harmonizations, developed through a temporal scheme." Although a prose statement about a poem may follow a logical pattern, the poem itself seldom does, for a poem is itself an action and not a statement about action. Ransom's description of the dual nature of poetry suggests too obviously to Brooks the age-old dichotomy of form and content and may lead to the erroneous conclusion that a poem consists of a "prose sense decorated by a sensuous imagery." An idea may be extracted from a poem by paraphrase, but its importance as far as the poem is concerned lies in its "dramatic propriety," in its relation to the total context of the poem. The conclusion of a poem is the "working out of the various tensions—set up by whatever means—by propositions, metaphors, symbols." The unity of a poem, therefore, is achieved by a dramatic, not a logical process. His definition of structure differs from Ransom's:

> The structure meant is a structure of meanings, evaluations, and interpretations; and the principle of unity which informs it seems to be one of balancing and harmonizing connotations, attitudes, and meanings. But even here one needs to make important qualifications: the principle is not one which involves the arrangement of the various elements into homogeneous groupings, pairing like with like. It unites the like with the unlike. It does not unite them, however, by the simple process of allowing one connotation to cancel out another nor does it reduce the contradictory attitudes to harmony by a process of subtraction. The unity is not a unity of the sort to be achieved by the reduction and simplification appropriate to an algebraic formula. It is a positive unity, not a negative; it represents not a residue but an achieved harmony.[17]

17. Cleanth Brooks, *The Well Wrought Urn: Studies in the Structure of Poetry* (New York, 1947), 193.

To think of a poem as a statement—and here he may be thinking of Ransom's assertion that the structure of a poem includes its paraphrasable content—sets up a false dilemma. The critic must avoid any kind of critical principle which suggests that the "prose sense" of a poem is a "rack on which the stuff of the poem is hung." Instead he should think of the prose paraphrase as a scaffold thrown around a building and not a part of the building itself. "To repeat," Brooks concludes, "most of our difficulties in criticism are rooted in the heresy of the paraphrase. If we allow ourselves to be misled by it, we distort the relation of the poem to its 'truth,' we raise the problem of belief in a vicious and crippling form, we split the poem between its 'form' and its 'content.'"

Ransom's response to this argument is included in "Poetry: The Formal Analysis," which appeared in the Summer, 1947, *Kenyon Review*. The New Critics, he writes, have brought about a "linguistic revolution in [their] reading of poetry." Although he agrees in general with their intensive and analytical emphasis upon the "total connotation of words," he is also aware of some weaknesses in their approach. "The critic goes straight from one detail to another," he insists, "in the manner of the bee who gathers honey from the several blossoms as he comes to them, without noticing the bush which supports all the blossoms." In their intensive study of the *texture* of the poem, the critics have neglected its *structure*. They have shown us the "exciting turns of poetic language," but they have not been able to give us an acceptable definition of a poem. No one has done more than Brooks, he concludes, to establish this kind of criticism; no one has demonstrated more ingenuity than he in "reading the obscure meanings of many well known poems." The essays in *The Well Wrought Urn* indicate, furthermore, that Brooks is attempting to conceive of the unified poem. He does not succeed in this new role, however, because, though he has "various formulations" for the poem, the terms he uses to define the poem are themselves undefined. Brooks insists that the "unity of poetic language has the form and status of a verbal paradox," but paradox, Ransom argues, is a "provisional way of speaking." We are not content to leave a paradox as a final meaning. Either we resolve the paradox or we sense its solution, which we feel is too obvious to require formal statement.

In this essay, Ransom restates his agreement with Brooks that the meaning of a poem and that of its paraphrase are not the same because the paraphrase always reduces the text and leaves out some of its meaning. But a poem has two kinds of meaning: One is its "ostensible argument," which can be rendered by paraphrase, and the other is its "tissue of meaning," which cannot. Like a Freudian dream, a poem has both a "'manifest' and permissible" and a "'latent' and suspected" content. Not only is the paraphrase possible, but it is also useful because it "straightens out the text and prunes the meaning down." He explains when and how the reader may find the paraphrase useful. If the literary text is long and involved, the paraphrase will assist him in getting "perspective and proportion." But, Ransom cautions, the critic must never think his work is done when he has made the paraphrase, even of the most difficult poem. Some texts do not demand a paraphrase because the reader receives their meaning intuitively and immediately. The serious reader of poetry, he concludes, will realize that a "poem is not included in its paraphrase," but a "poem must include its own paraphrase, or else a logical argument capable of being expressed in a paraphrase." After all, a poem is public property. It must "make contact with its auditors"; therefore it "must be decent enough to make formal sense."

Brooks addresses himself to this objection to his argument against paraphrase almost as if he had anticipated the very language in which Ransom would express his demurral. The reader must ask, he says, whether it is possible to frame a statement that will "say" briefly what the poem "says" as poem. If he had chosen, could not the poet have provided such a statement? Cannot the sensitive and intelligent reader frame such a statement?

> The answer must be that the poet himself obviously did not—else he would not have had to write his poem. We as readers can attempt to frame such a proposition in our effort to understand the poem; it may well help toward an understanding. Certainly, the efforts to arrive at such propositions can do no harm *if we do not mistake them for the inner core of the poem*—if we do not mistake them for "what the poem *really* says." For, if we take one of them to represent the essential poem, we have to disregard the qualifications exerted by

the total context as of no account, or else we have assumed that we can reproduce the effect of the total context in a condensed prose statement.[18]

In "The Concrete Universal: Observations on the Understanding of Poetry, I" (1954), Ransom returns to this discussion of the value of paraphrase. First of all, he would like to withdraw his statement made fifteen years or so earlier that a poem has both a logical structure and a texture "whose character was partly irrelevant to the logical form and purpose." Now he would say that the poem is an organism with three organs: the head, the heart, and the feet. Each organ speaks a different language: "the head in an intellectual language, the heart in an affective language, the feet in a rhythmical language." The language of the head presents an intellectual action; therefore the poem will have a beginning, a middle, and an end. In a complex modern poem the reader may not be sure of these respective parts, so he performs first an *explication de texte* and "then a translation of the composite language into the exclusive language of the intellect, which we call the logical paraphrase." Then Ransom asks, what is the use of this paraphrase?

> I think perhaps I used to make it a point of honor to intimate that the intellectuals with their paraphrases were abusing and spoiling our poems. But now I think that may be arrogant and wrong, and surely it is unreasonable and vain. There is nowhere in the world for the logical paraphrase to have come from except the poem, where it is implicit; and it is the intellectuals (in their capacity of formal logicians) who are masters of the science of explicating what is implicit. Nor do they harm the poem by taking their use of it. When we look again, the poem is still there, timeless and inviolable, for the other uses.[19]

In "Why Critics Don't Go Mad," Ransom says the particular fascination with Brooks's view of poetry is its nearness to the "ancient doctrine of divine inspiration." For Brooks, the poem exists in its metaphors; all else is insignificant. His approach to a poem is to go directly to the "'dominating' figure," to a "paradox or an

18. *Ibid.*, 206.
19. John Crowe Ransom, "The Concrete Universal: Observations on the Understanding of Poetry, I," *Kenyon Review*, XVI (Autumn, 1954), 554–64.

irony which is vivid" and which is likely to have "philosophical or religious implications." Then he wrestles as "much of the poem as possible" under this central figure and therein is the essential sense of the poem. He does not "want the poem to have a formal shape, but simply to unfold its own metaphorical energy." Although Ransom agrees with Brooks that the "poetic object must be defended in its full and private being," he also insists that the critic must define that "character in the poem which makes it discourse." The poem has "generality and definition," it is a "species of Aristotelian discourse," and it has a beginning, middle, and end if the argument is large enough to include these characteristics; if not, it has a "point," an "act of predication," and "that minute kind of order which we call syntax." The metaphors in the poem have to accommodate themselves to this much "logical formalism." Finally, Ransom suggested to Brooks that both of them might have been wrong all these years about the essential nature of a poem:

> A little while ago I was urging [Brooks] to accept the logical form of the poem as something fixed and . . . invincible; which the showy metaphors, episodic or "dominant" as they might be, had better make their peace with . . . and I had the idea of a poem as a great "paradox," a construct looking two ways, with logic trying to dominate the metaphors, and metaphors trying to dominate the logic. . . . But now I suggest that we must reckon with the meters too, and the poem assumes the form of a trinitarian existence. For the meters in turn enforce themselves against the logic and the metaphors, but against resistance.[20]

When one looks back through the critical writing of Brooks and Ransom, he is impressed with the number of similarities in their theories. Both men insist that literary criticism is an aesthetic criticism; no other approach is valid—not psychological, humanist, or Marxist. Both deplore the affective fallacy and argue that the intention of the poet is of little consequence. The critic must examine the poem itself, and this examination should concentrate on its form or structure. Ransom would surely have applauded this statement by Brooks: "If the artistic form, the

---

20. Ransom, "Why Critics Don't Go Mad," 159–68.

dramatic structure of the poem, defines, fortifies, and validates what the poet has to say—if the poet speaks to us more meaningfully when he speaks as artist through the medium of his poetic form, then we will do well to take into account the niceties of that form if we want to know precisely what he has to tell us."

Both Ransom and Brooks agree on the cognitive function of poetry. Poetry provides a means through which man can know a great deal that science cannot teach him. "Poetry," Ransom argued, "intends to recover the denser and more refractory original world which we know loosely through our perceptions and memories." In an unpublished book-length essay, the chief concerns of which can be reconstructed from his correspondence with Allen Tate, Ransom described this cognitive function. There are, he wrote Tate on September 5, 1926, three moments "in the historical order of experience." The first is the experience itself, which is "pure of all intellectual content, unreflective, concrete, and singular." The second is a period of thought, analysis, and application. During this period a record is made and concepts are formed; abstract ideas are conceived by subtracting "from the whole" experience. The third moment is one of reflection; it begins with memory and a sense of loss. "We become aware of the deficiency of the record. Most of experience is quite missing from it." When one realizes that the abstract ideas do not reproduce the initial experience, the sense of loss may become so acute that he will attempt to recapture that elusive first moment through an act of creation. Thus he may construct dreams, fancies, morals, art, or religion. All of these employ images, but these images exist alongside the previously conceived concepts. This "mixed world" is presented in all its complexity through this combination of ideas and images of "the conceptual and formal and the individual and concrete." From this pronouncement of a theory of poetic knowledge, Ransom moved easily to his statement of preference for the poetry that presents the opposition and then the reconciliation of the concept and the concrete image. Physical poetry is about things and Platonic poetry is about ideas; only metaphysical poetry introduces a "miracle," a figure that combines conceptual speculation and the concrete particularity of the world's body. This miraculism "arises when the poet discovers by analogy an identity between objects which is partial, though it should be considerable, and proceeds to an identification which is complete."[21]

With much of this mode of thought Brooks would certainly agree, as indicated in his discussion of the poem as an imitation of reality, a presentation of a unified experience:

> It is not enough for the poet to analyze his experience as the scientist does, breaking it up into parts, distinguishing part from part, classifying the various parts. His task is finally to unify experience. He must return to us the unity of the experience itself as man knows it in his own experience. The poem, if it be a true poem, is a simulacrum of reality—in this sense, at least, it is an "imitation"—by *being* an experience rather than any mere statement about experience or any mere abstraction from experience.[22]

But it is surely wrong to conceive of Brooks's criticism as a mere copy of that of his older contemporary. The reader who makes an intensive examination of their critical writings will be more impressed by their differences than by their similarities. Brooks is basically a practical critic. Although he does engage in theoretical speculations on the nature and function of poetry, he theorizes only to the extent necessary to provide a base for his commentary on individual poems. He has expressed his dislike of being known as "an indefatigable exegete," but the truth of the matter is that he is probably best known for his stimulating and illuminating analyses of significant literary works. If he, in Ransom's words, is "the most forceful and influential critic" of his generation, this reputation rests in large part on the fact, to quote Ransom again, that "he is the best reader of difficult verse around." Ransom obviously believed that Brooks's analytical criticism furnishes many examples of how poetry should be read, but he himself wrote few detailed commentaries of individual poems. In spite of a few glaring exceptions to this statement (one thinks immediately of "Yeats and His Symbols" and "Shakespeare at Sonnets"), most of Ransom's critical energy was expended in philosophical speculation on the nature and function of poetry. It is ironic that he was a critic who abhorred the kind of abstraction essential to philosophic exploration, one who

---

21. Young and Core (eds.), *Selected Letters of John Crowe Ransom*, 155–56; Ransom, "Poetry: A Note in Ontology," 111–39.
22. Brooks, *The Well Wrought Urn*, 212–13.

in poetry demanded the specific and concrete; nevertheless he was convinced that criticism must become more philosophical if it is to encompass the vast range of human experience that only art can render. Ransom set out to broaden and deepen the base of literary criticism, to provide it with an ontology that would enable it to deal meaningfully and systematically with the aspects of human behavior revealed in the art object. It is for this reason that he was critical of the formal critic who did his verbal analysis and stopped. Although he believed that a close reading of the text must precede any other critical operation, he insisted that a critic's job goes beyond exegesis.

In spite of his assertion that Brooks's defense of poetry rests on some "fairly impenetrable esoteric quality" when it should be defended because "of its human substance and on the naturalistic level," Ransom approved of the younger critic's insistence that poetry is a means of perception and cognition. It is not primarily a vehicle through which a poet may express emotion, feelings, or moralistic attitudes. But, if the two critics agreed on the function of poetry, they disagreed on its nature. Brooks argues that the coherence of a poem depends not upon logic but upon an attitude given life in a poem by its dominant metaphor. Ransom insisted that a metaphor cannot be a whole poem; neither can its unity depend upon the attitude embodied in the metaphor. The unity of the poem, Ransom argued, comes through an ideational core set against the metaphor, whereas Brooks believes that the unity of a poem "lies in the unification of attitudes into a hierarchy subordinated to a local and governing attitude." Thus, he insists that the unity of a poem is achieved through a dramatic process and not a logical one. Ransom held the contrary view.

This difference of opinion regarding the means by which a unified poem is formed probably accounts for the different demands Ransom and Brooks make upon the metaphor. Ransom insisted that there be a single and consistent development of the metaphorical comparison because the way in which the figure is developed often reveals the emotions of the poet. Brooks's demands are less rigid, allowing some "emotive meanderings," to use James E. Magner's phrase, as long as these seeming digressions contribute to the dominant tone of the poem. Ransom expected consistent development of the metaphor in order to give the poem logical completeness; only through this kind of development, he insisted, can a poet give his creation a stable and unified structure. Brooks does not believe a metaphor has to be made to conform to any "prose line of . . . argument"; there may and should be associative meanderings as long as they contribute to the central attitude of the poem. Brooks would say that the strength of a poem comes from the force of its tone and attitude; Ransom, from its consistent and logical development.

But these differences, though significant, are not irreconcilable. Both critics try to reach the same goal but from slightly different directions. They both would argue that the "rich and contingent materiality" of an experience cannot be explained in scientific terms and that the purpose of poetry is to do what science cannot: to render the experience, not to comment on it. For both, poetry is a profoundly serious activity that should attract, in its creation and consumption, the best minds of this, or any other, generation. As long as poetry is regarded as a trifling fiction, of no real use when compared to the demonstrated "truths" of the physical and social sciences, it will continue to be ignored and its creators regarded as eccentric misfits in the social order. Several years ago, Donald Davidson warned us that no civilization has ever lived without poetry and that ours can hardly be an exception. Few men in this century have contributed more energy or more genius than Ransom and Brooks in an attempt, if not to avoid, at least to postpone that tragedy. If Ransom attempted to convince us that poetry is valuable because it contains truths that are otherwise unavailable, Brooks has demonstrated how these truths may be recognized.

(1976)

John Crowe Ransom:
A Major Minor Poet

ALMOST everyone who has written about the poetry of John Crowe Ransom has commented upon the limitations he has imposed upon himself. Most of his important poetry was written in a period of eleven years, between 1916 and 1927; and two of these years were spent in military service. In his entire career, Ransom has published only 152 poems; his *Selected Poems* (1969) contains 72 poems, of which 8 are printed in an "original" and a "final" version, in what he calls "Sixteen Poems in Eight Pairings." Most of his poetic activity during the past forty-odd years, then, has been devoted to what he once called "tinkering" with his verse. Since 1927, he has published only 5 new poems, but he has altered, to a greater or lesser degree, almost all of the older ones and rewritten completely 8 of them.[1]

But Ransom, as Allen Tate has pointed out, limited the scope of his poems in more ways than one. When Tate says his old friend has always considered himself as "deliberately minor," one is reminded of Ransom's comments on "minor poems" in "Shakespeare at Sonnets":

> The virtue of formal lyrics, or "minor poems," is one that no other literary type can manifest: they are the only complete and self-determined poetry. There the poetic object is elected by a free choice from all objects in the world, and this object, deliberately elected and carefully worked up by the adult poet, becomes his microcosm. With a serious poet each minor poem may be a symbol of a major decision. It is as ranging and comprehensive an action as the mind has ever tried.

This essay originally appeared, in slightly different form, in *Spectrum*, III (June, 1972), 37–47. Reprinted by permission of the editor and Georgia State University.

1. John Crowe Ransom, *Selected Poems* (3rd ed.; New York, 1969). All references to Ransom's poetry are to this edition.

What Ransom means by "minor poems" will be understood by anyone who has read very widely in twentieth-century verse. In "The Metaphysical Poets," T. S. Eliot says modern poetry must be complex because "our civilization comprehends great variety and complexity and this variety and complexity, playing upon refined sensibility, must produce various and complex results. The poet must become more and more comprehensive, more allusive, more indirect, in order to force, to dislocate if necessary, language into meaning." The mode of the poet, then, must be ironic, and the essential ingredient of his verse, wit. This combination, Eliot's well-known argument continues, has not existed in English verse since the seventeenth century. Properly used, as in the poetry of Andrew Marvell, wit is a "structural decoration of a serious idea" or an "alliance of levity and seriousness." In poetry in which wit is not found—in most of that produced in the nineteenth century for example—a kind of immaturity is found.[2]

This discussion resembles the reasoning Ransom employs in his essay "Thoughts on the Poetic Discontent," which appeared in the *Fugitive* for June, 1925. There Ransom argues that "irony may be regarded as the ultimate mode of the great minds—it presupposes the others." Then he traces man's development from a naïve dualism, which leads him to suppose he controls the world in which he lives; through a kind of optimistic monism, based on the conviction that a benevolent God is personally responsible for assigning both man and nature appropriate places in a system "where not a sparrow falls without effect"; to the third and final stage where this romantic system falls under the "sober observations" of modern science. In his third stage there is a reaffirmation of dualism, this time of a different sort, for now the dualism is no longer "naive" and "unqualified"; it is "matured and informed." If the poetry of Wordsworth, Shelley, Tennyson, and Browning belongs to the "naive and uninformed" stage, that of Chaucer, Shakespeare, Donne, and Milton returns to the "stubborn fact of dualism with a mellow wisdom which we

---

2. Allen Tate, "For John Crowe Ransom at Seventy-Five," *Shenandoah*, XIV (Spring, 1963), 8; John Crowe Ransom, "Shakespeare at Sonnets," in Ransom, *The World's Body* (New York, 1938), 271–72; T. S. Eliot, "The Metaphysical Poets," in Eliot, *Homage to John Dryden: Three Essays on Seventeenth Century Poetry* (London, 1927), 31; T. S. Eliot, "Andrew Marvell," in Eliot, *Homage to John Dryden*, 38.

may call irony." And this irony is the "ultimate mode of the great minds [because] it presupposes all the others." It is the "rarest of the states of mind, because it is the most inclusive; the whole mind has been active in arriving at it, both creation and criticism, both poetry and science."[3]

Robert Penn Warren, in the earliest of the important critical essays about Ransom, pointed out that "wit and irony are the two properties most generally ascribed to his poetry." After this declaration, which sets the pattern of much of the later commentary, Warren demonstrates, by contrasting metaphor and wit, how wit and irony operate at the very center of Ransom's verse:

> Metaphor, we are told, implies a comparison which, on actual basis and according to strict science, is not defensible, but which justifies itself in terms of the emotional enrichment of a poetic theme, or more ambitiously sometimes, as the vehicle of its communication. Now wit is a critical and intellectual quality; when it appears in a poem, that poem, if otherwise successful as poetry, is enriched but in another direction.

Although wit may assist in resolving the theme of a poem, its principal function is to attempt to fuse the "emotional and the intellectual or critical qualities in poetry." The instrument of wit in Ransom's poetry, Warren concludes, is employed in "incidental imagery, in a certain pedantry of rhetoric, or in the organization of the entire material," but its most important use is to create "a specific and constant effect," and this effect is irony. "I hope," Warren concludes, "that by this time I shall have been anticipated by those readers familiar with Ransom's poetry in the definition of its center. It is to be defined in terms of that sensibility whose decay Ransom . . . has bewailed."[4]

These convictions and the attitudes they have fostered have created a special style in Ransom's verse, a style best characterized I think in the phrase "nuanced ambiguity," one which comes from the poet's conviction of the necessity of a double vision and his habit of saying one thing and implying another. In his criticism, Ransom has delineated three types of poetry—physical, Platonic, and metaphysical—and has indicated his fondness for

---

3. John Crowe Ransom, "Thoughts on the Poetic Discontent," *Fugitive*, IV (June, 1925), 63–64.

4. Robert Penn Warren, "John Crowe Ransom: A Study in Irony," *Virginia Quarterly Review*, XI (January, 1935), 100–103.

the last. Only in metaphysical poetry, he argues, is there perfect fusion of intellect and feeling. Ransom the poet and Ransom the critic are remarkably similar: The critic demands and the poet presents a poetry of logical rigor, structural discipline, and systematic presentation.

This orderliness of mind and precision of expression have enabled Ransom to compose a small number of poems, perhaps ten or twelve, that are, in the words of Randall Jarrell, "perfectly realized and occasionally almost perfect." It is significant, I think, that Jarrell suggests that Ransom's poetry should be compared to that of such great minor lyricists as Wyatt, Campion, and Marvell. For, as I indicated earlier, Ransom has imposed upon his poetry some rather strenuous limitations, not only upon the quantity of the verse he has allowed to stay in print but also upon both the matter and the manner of the poems he has published. Allen Tate says, as I have already pointed out, that Ransom has always considered himself "deliberately minor," and the meaning Tate intends that phrase to carry is indicated in a letter he wrote, on May 14, 1926, to Donald Davidson. Following his lifelong practice of getting Tate's reactions to his poems before they were published, Davidson had sent his old friend two sections of the long poem that appeared the next year as *The Tall Men* and had asked for Tate's comments and criticism. Tate's response bears directly on the matter under consideration:

> You asked for my criticism, criticism of these poems must certainly refer to your previous work in lyrical poetry, and I prefer the latter. I'm afraid Eliot is about right in saying there are no important themes for modern poets. Hence we all write lyrics; we must be subjective. I doubt if it were wholly due to a personal richness of mind— Milton's deliberate casting about for subjects; the English mind was more fertile then. I am convinced that Milton himself could not write a *Paradise Lost* now. Minds are less important for literature than cultures; our minds are as good as they ever were, but our culture is dissolving. . . . Something happened to us in Arnold's time. . . .
> I think there is one fundamental law of poetry, and it is negative: you can't *create* a theme.[5]

5. Randall Jarrell, "John Ransom's Poetry," *Sewanee Review*, LVI (Summer, 1948), 388; Tate, "For John Crowe Ransom at Seventy-Five," 8; John Tyree Fain and Thomas Daniel Young (eds.), *The Literary Correspondence of Donald Davidson and Allen Tate* (Athens, Ga., 1974), 166.

That Davidson did not accept Tate's criticisms entirely is demonstrated by the fact that he completed and published the long poem, which at that time Tate was calling "Your Tennessee Faust," and by a comment Davidson wrote in the fly leaf of *Homage to John Dryden,* apparently written while he was preparing his review of this book for the *Fugitive:*

> What Eliot is really justifying in Marvell is "minor" poetry—poetry that is content with narrow limits of form, few subjects, in order that it may perfectly succeed.[6]

The exchange of letters between Tate and Davidson and Tate and Ransom, written in the late twenties and the early thirties, continues their discussion of the kind and scope of subject available to the poet in the twentieth century. Davidson's views are expressed in a paragraph he quotes from F. Cudworth Flint:

> They [the modern poets] give us excellent lyrics, excellent narratives, excellent meditations; but what our culture chiefly needs at present is an artistic focal point, a center of unity, more *formally* evident than can be supplied by a collection of short poems. . . . [W]e not only need beliefs, of which we have almost too many . . . we also need a mythology, and a mythology credible, and capable of being embodied in poetry of *epic* magnitude.[7]

The following year, in a letter to John Hall Wheelock, Davidson discusses some of the important differences between his theory of poetry and that of Ransom and Tate, and this statement helps to define the term *minor poetry* as I am using it here. "Their procedure"—that is, the procedure of Ransom and Tate—Davidson wrote, "was to seek out ways of making the 'small' poem carry a tension that would charge it heavily with meaning. Implied in their practice—though not clearly stated in their critical pronouncements—was the belief that the poem of large meaning and extended dimensions was impossible for a modern to execute. Therefore they did not attempt narrative verse on any but the smallest possible scale and in general avoided any sustained efforts in verse."[8]

---

6. Fain and Young (eds.), *Literary Correspondence of Donald Davidson and Allen Tate,* 170.

7. F. Cudworth Flint, "Five Poets," *Southern Review,* I (April, 1936), 674.

8. Fain and Young (eds.), *Literary Correspondence of Donald Davidson and Allen Tate,* 186.

Ransom's theories of the nature and functions of poetry persuaded him that as poet he could perform best in what we are calling a minor mode. As early as 1926, in a series of letters to Allen Tate, Ransom proposed what he was later to call the ontological significance of poetry. Through a combination of images and concepts, poetry can present the concrete particularities of an experience and show the reality of an object's being in a way that science cannot. But, if one may judge from Ransom's actual practice, the "concrete particularities of an actual experience" can best be presented in poetry of a certain type. The recurring themes in Ransom's verse are those that have concerned man almost as far into the past as history reaches: man's dual nature, the conflict of body and soul, mutability, the awesome certainty of death, and the passing of youthful beauty and energy, the disparity between man's hopes and what he can reasonably expect to accomplish. Along with these universal themes appear others that are more modern. Many of Ransom's protagonists, as Warren has pointed out, suffer from a dissociation of sensibility, from a schism between reason and imagination, between science and faith.

The style of the mature verse is as unique and unusual as the subject matter is typical and commonplace. It is a highly personal style imbued with a remarkable consistency of tone: The subtle irony, the nuanced ambiguities, the conceits, the wit, and the cool detached tone are the elements one associates with Ransom. Even more significant, perhaps, for our present purpose is Ransom's use of the simple narrative, the fable, or the anecdote as a means of presenting the "constant actuals"; the usual situation is that of the innocent or naïve character who becomes involved in a rather commonplace situation. Because of this involvement he comes to have a fuller understanding of his own nature and the nature of the world in which he lives. Because of the death of his neighbor's daughter, a man is made to ponder the inscrutability of the world; a young friar walks on a battlefield after a battle and is left to contemplate reality as a puzzling maze of irreconcilable opposites; a young girl is brought face to face with the reality of death, the most painful and pervasive fact of human existence, through the death of her pet hen. But these "massive and ineluctable facts," as Graham Hough says, are always presented in "delicate settings," a simple little fable seldom running to more than twenty or thirty lines.[9]

Ransom's dissatisfaction with the poetry included in his first volume, *Poems About God* (1919), is well known. From *Grace After Meat*, which Robert Graves brought out in England, to the publication of *Selected Poems* (1969), Ransom had not allowed a single poem from his first book to appear in print. This last book contains only one poem, "Overtures," and that one is included, I am tempted to say, in order for Ransom to comment specifically on *why* it no longer pleases him. In his commentary following "Overtures," Ransom says he had promised himself never to republish any of the *Poems About God* because of the "general poverty of its style and its blatant and inconsistent theologizing." Although his "theologizing" is never again so open and direct, this first collection introduces the several themes that reappear in Ransom's mature poetry, including mutability and the grief that comes to man because he cannot or will not accept the duality of his nature. The poet's dissatisfaction with his early verse, then, would seem to be not as much with its theologizing as with the poverty of its style, with its flat and trite diction, its pat and too-obvious irony, and its often sentimental tone. The manner of the later poetry is markedly different from that of the early, for the later contains that "mellow wisdom" which Ransom calls irony, the "ultimate mode of great minds."[10] And, along with the irony, there is its constant companion wit, attempting to fuse the "emotional and intellectual qualities" of the verse. But most of all, the later poems—though small in scope and severely limited in subject matter, though written in a mode deliberately minor—are heavily charged with meaning. Properly read, these poems can inform us of the full range of our limitations and our potentialities in a way no other instrument can.

The poem that Ransom read to his fellow Fugitives during the winter of 1922, and the one which convinced Tate that "overnight . . . [Ransom] had left behind him the style of his first book

---

9. John Crowe Ransom, "The Poet and the Critic," *Southern Review*, n.s., I (January, 1965), 14.
10. Ransom, *Selected Poems*, 14; Ransom, "Thoughts on the Poetic Discontent," 64.

and, without confusion, had mastered a new style," was "Necrological."[11] A brief look at this poem will demonstrate, I think, Ransom's almost uncanny ability to put "massive facts in small or delicate settings," to charge a simple little fable with the inexhaustible ambiguities, the paradoxes and tensions, the dichotomies and ironies that make up the life of man in the twentieth century.

Suggested by a reading of the death of Charles the Bold of Burgundy, who after being slain in battle was left to be eaten by the wolves, this poem relates, in what appears to be a straightforward and uncomplicated manner, an unusual view of this horrible incident. At dawn on the day following a rather bloody battle, a young friar says his "paternosters duly," "scourged his limbs," and goes out on the battlefield to see if he can clear his head because with "much riddling" it has become "unruly."[12] In the first light of the morning, he can see the many corpses left from the previous day; he notes that only the dead are left because the living have gone to celebrate their victory. But it is easy to die, he thinks; the ambiguous nature of this statement, which on the surface seems so simple and direct, becomes obvious later in the poem.

He notes that the dead wear no "raiment against the air," that Bartholomew's men "had spoiled them where they fell." In the unclear light of early dawn, the white flesh of the naked bodies dots the landscape like the blossoms of the asphodel. But not all the bodies are white; some are "gory and fabulous"; these are those whom the sword has pierced and the "grey wolf eaten." The friar is momentarily shocked by this gruesome sight, but like many of the rest of us he calms himself by offering a too-easy solution to a very knotty problem. Such, he reasons, is the expected end to a hero's life: He who seeks glory must face danger and he who lives constantly with danger must expect sometime to be defeated. In battle, men die and the bodies of those who are killed, if unattended to, will be ravaged by nature. On this day Bartholomew was the victor, so he has left his foes on

11. Allen Tate, *"The Fugitive, 1922–25," Princeton Library Chronicle,* III (April, 1942), 78.

12. Quotations from "Necrological" are taken from Ransom's *Selected Poems,* 42–43.

the battlefield, "prone and shattered"; but destiny makes all even: those who won today go to lose their life tomorrow on another battlefield.

After this rather generalized view, the friar's attention is focused upon three specific scenes. In the first, beneath the "blue ogive of the firmament" he sees a dead warrior whose knees are embraced by his leman. This young girl, we learn, "with her flame had warmed his tent" and for him she had endured "all men's pleasantries." With this observation, the poem takes a turn. The friar begins to realize that these bodies do not represent abstract "casualties" (Ransom says his earliest memory was a rage against abstraction); they are dead human beings with passions and desires, hopes and expectations other than those one associates with the chivalric knight. This significant distinction is considerably strengthened in the next scene: By the dark water he sees a white horse with his thrown rider lying nearby. "The great beast had spilled there his little brain, / And the little groin of the knight was spilled by a stone." This comparison of the man and his great stallion makes the humanness of the knight even more real to the friar.

The final scene demonstrates Ransom's use of language to create the precise tone he is seeking. Language which on the surface seems most inappropriate becomes both appropriate and effective in the context in which it appears:

> The youth possessed him then of a crooked blade
> Deep in the belly of a lugubrious wight;
> He fingered it well, and it was cunningly made;
> But strange apparatus was it for a Carmelite.

Like many of Ransom's other poems, "Necrological" ends somewhat inconclusively. The friar is not able to digest immediately the impressions he has had. But when one reflects upon the poem, he can see that the seemingly vague ending is the result of the friar's asking himself some tough questions, some of which have no pat answers. Of one thing, though, we are absolutely certain: the friar is not the same man he was when he came upon this battlefield.

> Then he sat upon a hill and bowed his head
> As under a riddle, and in a deep surmise

So still that he likened himself unto those dead
Whom the kites of heaven solicited with sweet cries.

The experiences of this day are traumatic. We observed the friar at the moment before he alters the manner in which he views the cosmos. As Robert Buffington has pointed out, "he is a monist at the point of becoming a dualist."[13] One approach to the poem is to see the friar's conflict in terms of the age-old debate between body and soul. The "deep surmise" in which we leave the friar is the result of his realizing that his monistic system offers no satisfactory solution to the many obvious paradoxes he discovers on the battlefield, and the battlefield is, of course, a microcosm of the world. The body is more than a mere enclosure for the soul, and there is a kind of love far different from the divine adoration the friar feels for his Lord. He wonders if he is denying a part of his nature, if his celibate love comprehends the feeling of the "leman" whose "flame had warmed" the tent of her lover.

The dilemma of the friar is that of modern man. Like the protagonist in Ransom's poem "Man Without Sense of Direction," the friar can neither "fathom nor perform" his nature. Devout and learned though he is, he finds it most difficult to relate his faith in an all-powerful and all-merciful God to the facts of the real world around him. Can one justify the suffering and death that have occurred on this field? Is there any reason for human affection if the relationship between man and woman will end as did the one between the "leman" and her lover? How can one justify sacrifice and devotion to a sacred cause if the victor in this day's battle goes to meet death in tomorrow's?

In this, the first of his mature poems, Ransom demonstrates one of the perennial arguments of his criticism: A poem can express truth that transcends the facts of science. The relatively innocent friar becomes involved in what could have been a rather commonplace situation, but because of this involvement he acquires knowledge he could have gotten in no other way. At the end of the poem he is a far wiser, if sadder, man than he was at the beginning. He has a fuller understanding of his nature and of the nature of the world in which he *must* live. He sees the vast

---

13. Robert Buffington, *The Equilibrist: A Study of John Crowe Ransom's Poems, 1916–1963* (Nashville, 1967), 401.

chasm that often separates what man wants—and maybe what he needs—and what he can get. Although the friar knows, he does not act. When we last see him, he is so still "that he likened himself unto those dead / Whom the kites of heaven solicited with sweet cries." The friar may yearn for an ideal world in which he can escape the constant struggle between the two sides of his nature, but he knows he must live in the real world—one in which brave, loyal, and dedicated men are killed and devoured by wolves or one in which the best and strongest live only to die tomorrow or the day after. The friar, then, is left contemplating reality as irreconcilable opposites, and he is as incapable of action as the problem that plagues him is incapable of solution.

In this poem, as in other of his near-perfect lyrics, Ransom has been content with severe restrictions on both his form and his subject matter. Consequently, his execution must approach perfection, for in such small compass one blemish would be most obvious. Although the poem is modest in length and scope, it is heavily charged with meaning. Its theme can be universally applied; the friar is rendered impotent by one of the oldest and the most persistent of the insoluble problems that man has learned to live with. The age in which he has lived may have denied Ransom a "mythology credible . . . in poetry of *epic* magnitude," but in a small handful of poems he has provided, as Isabel Gambel MacCaffrey points out, "an accurate mirror of the modern sensibility. In it are reflected the miraculous virtues of contemporary verse at its best: its combination of delicacy with strength, of fervor with restraint, of elegance with earthiness."[14] In his criticism, Ransom has argued that, properly read, poetry can furnish illuminating insight into the nature of man and the nature of the world in which he lives. The best of Ransom's poems will be read as long as poetry is regarded as a serious art, because in them one acquires with great pleasure that kind of knowledge that he can get almost nowhere else.

(1972)

14. Flint, "Five Poets," 674; Isabel Gambel MacCaffrey, "Ceremonies of Bravery," in Louis D. Rubin, Jr., and Robert D. Jacobs (eds.), *South: Modern Southern Literature in Its Cultural Setting* (Garden City, N.Y., 1961), 210.

Our Two Worthies: Robert Frost and John Crowe Ransom

WHEN John Crowe Ransom went overseas in the fall of 1917, he carried with him early drafts of many of the poems that were published two years later in *Poems About God*. His military duties demanded so much of his time and attention during the first few months of his assignment in France that he was able to do little writing. In the spring of 1918, however, after serving nearly four months at the front as an officer in the field artillery, he was reassigned to the base at Saumur. In his first tour of duty at this post, he had received instruction in the operation of the 155 Howitzer; in this second tour, he was to pass along the information he had received to the officers who were just beginning their tour of overseas service. During his two years in France, while his friend Christopher Morley was attempting to find a publisher for *Poems About God*, Ransom had given as much time and thought as he could to revising this early verse. Although Morley was trying to place individual poems with magazines at the same time he was searching for a publisher willing to bring out the first volume of an unknown poet, he was having little success. He placed one poem with the *Independent*, but at least a dozen other journals returned everything he sent them.

Partly because of the discouraging news he received from New York and partly because of his dissatisfaction with these early poems, Ransom decided that if a publisher were not found soon, he would withdraw the manuscript, completely revise it,

---

This essay originally appeared, in slightly different form, in *Frost: Centennial Essays II*, ed. Jac Tharpe (Jackson, Miss., 1976). Reprinted by permission of the University Press of Mississippi.

and send it out again when he returned to the States. He wrote Morley on May 13, 1918, that the volume was "clean done," that he had "outgrown" it, and that it had become "a bit artificial" with him.[1] Ransom requested that if Henry Holt, whom Morley planned to ask to reconsider the volume, turned it down, it be held for him to pick up when he came through New York after the war.

In the letter with these instructions, Ransom sent four new poems, many suggested changes in the old ones, and a most unusual introduction, one in which he indicated his dissatisfaction with the volume and hinted that it might soon be suppressed. As soon as Morley received this revised manuscript, he sent it to Henry Holt with his strong endorsement. What neither he nor Ransom could know was the identity of the reader to whom Holt would send the manuscript for an official reaction, a reader who would share Morley's genuine enthusiasm for the volume. At this time, Holt was paying Robert Frost a small retainer, and he was expected to read and evaluate any poetry manuscripts the company was considering for publication. One of the two or three requests Frost received for this service was for a report on *Poems About God*. His reaction strongly supported the endorsement of Morley, for, as he recalled many years later, the young Tennessee poet "had the art and . . . the tune."[2] Frost's recommendation, added to that of Morley, apparently persuaded the publisher to bring out, in those war years when the demand for poetry was very slow indeed, a volume of verse by an unknown poet.

Although some of the reviewers of *Poems About God* saw a strong influence of the New England poet in these poems about growing up in middle Tennessee around the turn of the century, Ransom said he had not read much of Frost until after the volume was published. In the years just before he began writing verse, Ransom read with great interest and enthusiasm the poetry of Robert Browning, A. E. Housman, and Thomas Hardy. These were the poets who influenced him most before he be-

---

1. John Crowe Ransom's letters to Christopher Morley are in the Haverford College Library.
2. Cleanth Brooks and Robert Penn Warren (eds.), *Understanding Poetry: An Anthology for College Students* (Rev. ed.; New York, 1950), 12.

came acquainted with the work of the French Symbolists immediately after World War I. When he returned to Nashville in 1919 and renewed his associations with the Fugitives, however, he began to read as much contemporary verse as he could. Among the poets he read then was Robert Frost, and he was somewhat envious, he said years later, of the New Englander's ability to write quality verse in a manner to appeal to the modern reader whose taste was shaped by popular fiction. He was one of the few American poets of his generation—the only one of consequence except E. A. Robinson and, perhaps, Edna St. Vincent Millay—in whose hands "poetry as a living art" had not "lost its public support."[3] Although evidently influenced by modernism, Frost had avoided the extremes found in the work of such "pure" poets as Wallace Stevens and such "obscure" poets as Allen Tate. He later did a complete about-face in his attitude toward T. S. Eliot, but in the mid-1920s he speculated that Eliot's poetry would not last. "The genius of our language," he wrote in the *Literary Review* for July 14, 1923, "is notoriously given to feats of hospitality; but it seems to me it will be hard pressed to find accommodations at the same time for two such incompatibles as Mr. Wordsworth and the present Mr. Eliot; and any realist must admit that what happens to be the prior tenure of the mansion in this case is likely to be stubbornly defended."

About two years later, Ransom wrote a short piece for the *Fugitive* in which he argued that irony is "the ultimate mode of the great minds" because "it is most inclusive" and because the "whole mind has been active in arriving at it, both creation and criticism, both poetry and science." Although the "trim and easy" poetry of Robert Frost is "anything but pretentious," it marks its author as modern because it "contains plenty of this irony." Its spirit goes back beyond the romantic poets of the nineteenth century to Donne and his contemporaries in the seventeenth. Frost's attitude toward nature is "immensely metaphysical":

> When this poet sees the bent birches in the wood, he "likes to think a boy's been swinging them," a hypothesis which would immediately put man and nature into sodality of merry play. But he is too skeptical to believe that; he is forced to consider that ice storms have bent

---

3. John Crowe Ransom, "Poets Without Laurels," in Ransom, *The World's Body* (New York, 1938), 55.

the birches, and thereupon his romantic impulse, baffled but not yet defeated, takes a new tack and begins to personalize the trees, imagined under their ice-coating. . . . Whenever he dwells on Nature, he is the same; as when he finds the rotting timbers attempting to warm the forest with the "slow smokeless burning of decay." It would indeed seem that Nature never otherwise puts in an appearance in human art—whether poetry or painting. Always the natural processes are personalized, and art consoles us with its implication of far-flung analogies between our order and the natural order. Mr. Frost is more than ordinarily delicate in making this implication.[4]

Despite his admiration for Frost's verse, Ransom's speculation on the nature of poetry, as well as his attempts to justify the existence of art to the members of a society whose compelling interests were almost entirely in material values, led him to defend a kind of poetry Frost seldom produced. Although he came to believe the term too restrictive, he called this kind of verse "metaphysical," and declared it "the most original and exciting, and intellectually perhaps the most seasoned, that we know in our literature." The staple of such poetry is the conceit, a "meant metaphor," one which is "developed so literally" and "predicated so baldly that nothing else can be meant." In this kind of poetry a "miraculism arises when the poet discovers by analogy an identity between objects which is partial, though it should be considerable, and proceeds to an identification which is complete."[5] This kind of poetry can be justified in a world dominated by science because it provides man with a kind of knowledge he can receive from no other source. His efforts to point up the differences between poetry and prose brought him to his well-known structure-texture formulation. In addition to a loose logical structure, "which is not so tight and precise on its logical side as a scientific or technical prose structure generally is," poetry, unlike prose, has an "irrelevant local texture." The structure includes the poem's logical content, with its beginning, middle, and end, its appropriately interspersed transitions, and its rhyme (if any) and meter. Although the poem's "determinate meaning" may be expressed by its paraphrasable content, its "in-

4. John Crowe Ransom, "Thoughts on the Poetic Discontent," *Fugitive*, IV (June, 1925), 63–64.

5. John Crowe Ransom, "Poetry: A Note in Ontology," in Ransom, *The World's Body*, 135, 137, 139.

determinate or final meaning" may be represented only by taking into consideration the "residue of meaning" which does not go into the logical paraphrase. This "residue of meaning" resides in the "irrelevant local texture"; that is, in diction, imagery, sound, and figurative language. In his theory as in his practice, then, Ransom was drawn toward what Donald Davidson has called the "packed line" with its "closely woven inferential and referential scheme." Although Ransom often insisted that the real value of a Frost poem was seldom enclosed within the apparently innocent simplicity of its paraphrasable content, he desired poetry with a textural richness that he seldom found in the poems of Frost. Obviously Ransom would agree with Eliot's explanation of why contemporary poetry must be difficult. "Our civilization comprehends great variety and complexity," Eliot wrote in "The Metaphysical Poets," and this variety and complexity, playing upon a refined sensibility, must produce various and complex results: "The poet must become more and more comprehensive, more allusive, more indirect, in order to force, to dislocate if necessary, language into meaning."[6]

Although Ransom concurred with Allen Tate in the conviction that Frost "wrote some of the finest poems of our time," he also agreed with that critic's statement that Frost was not "my kind of poet."[7] He simply did not believe that much of Frost's verse was of the sort designed to "realize the world," to enable the reader to see it better. But if Ransom's personal preferences did not make Frost's poetry appealing to him, he often said that his New England contemporary was making a valuable contribution to the cultural life of his time because Frost's public readings of his verse were the most successful example he knew of the serious artist attempting to bring his work to the people. Consequently, in the middle 1930s, when a committee of the Centennial Club of Nashville asked Ransom to recommend a poet to appear before that group, he presented, as his first choice among the several poets he suggested, the name of Robert Frost. After

6. John Crowe Ransom, "Wanted: An Ontological Critic," in Ransom, *The New Criticism* (Norfolk, Conn., 1941), 63–64; Donald Davidson, *Still Rebels, Still Yankees and Other Essays* (Baton Rouge, 1957), 7; T. S. Eliot, "The Metaphysical Poets," in Eliot, *Selected Essays* (New York, 1932), 248.
7. Allen Tate, *Memoirs and Opinions* (Chicago, 1975), 96.

Frost accepted, Ransom agreed to host a small dinner party in his honor and to introduce him before his reading to the club members and their guests. Although many well-known writers—including Witter Bynner, Louis Untermeyer, and John Gould Fletcher—were giving readings in Nashville during this period, no one attracted a crowd as large as that gathered to hear Frost. Every seat in the auditorium was taken, and a few latecomers were seated in the aisles or standing against the wall in the back. After Ransom's introduction, Frost read and commented on his poems (Donald Davidson said he chanted them, seldom referring to a manuscript) for almost two hours. No poet in their memory, Ransom and Davidson agreed, had ever been received so well by a Nashville audience. In addition to prolonged applause and a standing ovation at the end of the reading, Frost obviously had the complete attention of his audience for the entire time. His work was so well known that his announcement of the poem he was to read was often lost in a spontaneous burst of applause. Frost was understandably pleased by the reception he received, and he told Ransom and Davidson, who drove him to a party given for him following the reading, that the Fugitives had created in Nashville a "climate for poetry."

Everyone was in a good mood and the party went long beyond the time originally set for it. Frost's chair in the corner where he stationed himself shortly after his arrival was completely surrounded all night and conversation never waned. Davidson reported that the talk that evening was about as good as he had ever participated in, and Ransom thought Frost appeared "absolutely exhilarated." It was almost three o'clock, therefore, when Ransom set out to take their visitor back to his hotel. When they arrived there, both men were deeply involved in a discussion that they wished to continue; consequently Ransom parked his car and walked with Frost to the hotel. There before the front entrance—both still in tuxedos—and in the lobby, the two poets talked until daylight. Milkmen were on the street, Ransom recalled many years afterwards, before they went inside, and "there we stood in our dress clothes, in the morning sun, still talking. People passing by must have thought it funny." Just before he was due at school for an eight o'clock class, Ransom rushed home to change clothes. His wife, whom he had dropped off on his way downtown, was awakened and heard him complain as he searched for appropriate clothing, "I must go to class, but Robert Frost can sleep."[8]

What Ransom was not aware of at this time, of course, was that this association with Robert Frost very likely changed his entire future and placed him in such a position that he would have a significant effect on the course of American literature for two decades or more. Less than two years after he and Frost reluctantly broke off their conversation in the lobby of the Maxwell House, Ransom had moved from Nashville to Gambier, Ohio, and was deeply involved in planning the first issue of the *Kenyon Review*, which quickly became one of the most distinguished and influential journals of its time. He had left Vanderbilt after more than twenty years to join the faculty of Kenyon College because of a series of negotiations that had been set in motion by Robert Frost. In the spring of 1937, when Gordon Keith Chalmers was appointed president of Kenyon College, almost his first official act was to invite his old friend Robert Frost to join him as poet-in-residence. Chalmers and his wife, Roberta Teale Schwartz, the author of two books of poetry, wanted to establish at Kenyon a journal of the kind and quality of the *Yale Review* or the *Virginia Quarterly Review*, and they knew that having Frost's name associated with such a venture would go a long way toward assuring its success. But Frost did not wish to leave New England, nor did he want any kind of position that would impede his freedom of movement. His reputation was so firmly established that he was receiving more invitations to lecture or to read his poems than he could comfortably fill; therefore he refused Chalmers' offer. In declining, however, he suggested that the "man for the job might be available down there in Tennessee."[9] One cannot help wondering how much the pleasant memories of his visit to Nashville contributed to the warmth with which Frost recommended Ransom. Roberta Chalmers, who had published some of her first poems in the *Fugitive* and who was an admirer of Ransom's poetry, supported Frost's recommendation, and Chal-

---

8. Conversations with Donald Davidson, 1961 to 1964, and with John Crowe Ransom, 1976.

9. Conversations with Gordon Keith Chalmers, president of Kenyon College, and Roberta Teale Schwartz, spring, 1936.

mers came to Nashville to persuade Ransom to accept the position. This meeting occurred in the spring of 1937. Barely six months later, Chalmers and Ransom had begun to formulate plans for the *Review,* and a few years later they organized the Kenyon School of English. The impact of these two developments on the literary world was such that a small liberal arts college with little more than a local reputation for excellence soon became the focus of some of the most important literary activity that occurred in England and America for twenty years or more.

Once Ransom was settled in Gambier, the association between him and Frost continued without interruption. Frost came to Kenyon almost every spring to visit the Chalmers and often stayed for a week or longer. During these visits, he not only gave public readings, but he was also available for informal sessions with students and faculty. Since he and Frost were "in the same business," as Ransom said, they saw a good deal of each other. Often they appeared together on formal programs, and Ransom arranged as many occasions as he could to allow his students to meet their famous visitor. There were formal dinners at the Chalmers and elsewhere and many of a more private character, usually at the Ransoms or in the home of Philip Blair Rice, the associate editor of the *Review.* During the early 1940s, Ransom spent many of his summers in Middlebury, Vermont, as a member of the faculty of the Bread Loaf School of English. Among his most enjoyable experiences of these summers were the frequent visits of Robert Frost, who had a home just down the road from where Ransom and his family lived with other members of the summer school faculty. Once after dinner at the Ransoms, Robb Reavill Ransom recalled many years later, the two poets sat on the porch and talked until almost midnight. When Frost started home, Ransom offered to walk a part of the way with him. At Frost's gate, they paused and talked for a while. When Ransom started home, Frost accompanied him, and the two poets spent the remainder of the night walking from one gate to another, so engrossed in conversation they did not realize they had talked the night away until Mrs. Ransom called them in to breakfast. Frost was to be away for the summer of 1942, and he invited the Ransoms to live in his house, an arrangement which pleased Ransom very much because at meals in the living quarters supplied by the school he was expected to preside "over little tables of old maid students in the dining room." [10]

The close personal relationship between the two poets continued through the years, though few letters were exchanged, and Frost's opinion of Ransom's poetry did not change. In 1956, during one of his visits to Kenyon, he told a student audience, "You have right here on this campus the greatest living American poet." [11] As one might expect, the undergraduate writer who reported Frost's statement took exception to it, insisting that the person deserving that honor was the speaker.

But Ransom was never able, apparently, to make up his mind completely about Frost the poet. During the 1950s and after, he taught on several college campuses a course he called "Poetry of Our Own Age," and though he usually included a few poems by Frost, he concentrated on the poetry of T. S. Eliot and Wallace Stevens, in later years devoting more attention to W. H. Auden than he did to Frost. The rich evocative texture of the poetry of Eliot and Stevens, he told his classes, could fully engage the faculties of readers "fully aged in the academic disciplines" and assist them in realizing a world "made of whole and indefeasible objects." In 1961, when he was invited to offer a seminar in the poetry of Stevens and Eliot at Ohio State University, he was delighted to accept because the preparation for this assignment would require him to do some work he had intended to do for many years. Since completing *The New Criticism* twenty years before, he had wanted to write another extensive essay on Eliot, who he was convinced was the most important poet of his generation. On two previous occasions he had been less than generous in his comments on this poet, he said, and he wanted "to write him up" again so he could indicate formally his conviction of Eliot's greatness. He had also changed his mind about Stevens, whom once he had classified as "just below the rank of greatness," but whom he now regarded as a "major poet whose magnitude had only gradually dawned" upon him. Among the last of Ransom's essays were reappraisals of Eliot and Stevens, but he never wrote extensively about Frost, a poet whose achievement

10. Interview, Robb Reavill Ransom, February 12, 1971; conversation with John Crowe Ransom and Robb Reavill Ransom, 1976.
11. Interview, Perry Lentz and other members of the Kenyon College faculty, 1976.

he considered of lasting importance and a man whose companionship he cherished beyond almost all others. One explanation for this long silence may be included in a letter he wrote Allen Tate shortly after Frost's death: "I felt very sad about Frost, though I didn't go to the funeral. I generally had the curious feeling about him of being indebted to his achievement, in this sense: he was at his best a fine poet, but he chose not to be at his best generally, and therefore discharged the debt to the less literate society which we can't find in us to take seriously. That's a sort of missionary feeling, with relief that somebody else is doing the job."[12] That Ransom was never able to see the whole of Frost's greatness was, in part at least, the result of a consistent application of aesthetic principles developed by one of the most significant theoretical critics of this century. Except in a few poems, Frost did not produce the miraculism that Ransom sought in poetry.

(1976)

12. John Crowe Ransom, "The Planetary Poet," *Kenyon Review*, XXVI (Winter, 1964), 233; Thomas Daniel Young and George Core (eds.), *Selected Letters of John Crowe Ransom* (Baton Rouge, 1985), 405.

The Little Houses Against the Great

ON February 20, 1949, a committee composed of Allen Tate, Katherine Garrison Chapin, Katherine Anne Porter, Willard Thorp, Paul Green, Louise Bogan, T. S. Eliot, Theodore Spencer, Conrad Aiken, W. H. Auden, Karl Shapiro, Robert Lowell, and Léonie Adams awarded to Ezra Pound the Bollingen Prize for Poetry. This award, carrying with it a grant of one thousand dollars provided by the Bollingen Foundation, was given to the "author of that book of verse published during the previous calendar year which in the judgment of the Fellows in American Letters [of the Library of Congress] represented the highest achievement of American poetry during that year." Pound's award was for his *Pisan Cantos*. Attempting to anticipate an unfavorable reaction to an unpopular choice, the members of the committee who favored Pound's selection, including everyone except Karl Shapiro, issued a joint statement:

> The Fellows are aware that objections may be made to awarding a prize to a man situated as is Mr. Pound. In their view, however, the possibility of such an objection did not alter the responsibility assumed by the jury of selection. This was to make a choice for the award among the eligible books, provided any one merited such recognition, according to the stated terms of the Bollingen Prize. To permit other considerations than that of poetic achievement would destroy the significance of the award.[1]

On February 25, 1949, in a letter to the Baltimore *Sun*, Karl

---

This essay originally appeared, in slightly different form, in *Sewanee Review*, LXXXVIII (Spring, 1980). Reprinted by permission of the editor.

1. Most of the men on the committee were in their forties or fifties when the United States entered World War II; therefore they did not serve in the armed forces. Karl Shapiro, who cast the dissenting vote, was the only member to see active duty; he served in the European theater of operations from 1942 to 1945. He heard, therefore, some of Pound's anti-American broadcasts.

Shapiro stated his reasons for dissenting from the vote of the committee:

> I disagree vehemently with the principle embodied in the Library press release that to judge a work of art on other than esthetic grounds is "to deny the objective perception of value on which any civilized society must rest." This is not a statement of principle but an apology; in no case is it a fact that can stand historical or logical inquiry.... I think it can be pointed out that such an interpretation of literature stems directly from a coterie of writers called the "new critics."

Although Shapiro acknowledged that he found the *Pisan Cantos* "a work of extremely high order," his conviction of the function of literature in a democratic society would not allow him to award a literary prize to a poet intent on destroying that society. "Pound," Shapiro insisted, "has been a confessed Fascist and a violent anti-Semite for many years . . . [and] the values I perceive in the *Cantos* are the subjective values . . . of an embittered expatriate who turns world destroyer."

In April, 1949, the *Partisan Review* took exception to the vagueness of the committee's announcement, and William Barrett offered a satiric substitute for its statement, awarding the prize to Pound for his anti-Semitism. Barrett's accusation brought responses from Auden, Irving Howe, George Orwell, Tate, and others. Shapiro repeated his reason for voting against the *Pisan Cantos:* The literary quality of the work was "vitiated" by its subject. Tate responded twice: First he accused Barrett of insinuating that the committee was favorably influenced by Pound's anti-Semitic prejudice, and he demanded satisfaction. Apparently Tate wanted either a retraction or, better still, a duel. Then he replied more moderately and rationally, saying that Pound in the *Pisan Cantos* had fulfilled admirably the first obligation of the poet: to preserve the health and vitality of the language. (This response in expanded form became "Ezra Pound and the Bollingen Prize.")[2]

The most damaging reaction to the committee's decision, however, came in two articles by Robert Hillyer published in the June 11 and 18, 1949, issues of the *Saturday Review of Literature*.

---

2. Allen Tate, "Ezra Pound and the Bollingen Prize," in Tate, *The Man of Letters in the Modern World: Selected Essays, 1928–1955* (Cleveland, 1955), 264–67.

Hillyer had won the Pulitzer Prize for poetry for 1934, and he was now president of the Poetry Society of America and professor of English at Kenyon College. His argument against the decision of the committee follows fairly closely the lines of Shapiro's objections, though he disagrees violently that the *Pisan Cantos* possesses any literary merit. "I will say with full confidence," he begins, "that no one outside neoesthetic circles, who examines that opus, will fail to agree that if it be 'poetic achievement' then everything we have known as poetry in the English language from Chaucer to Frost is *not* poetic achievement." In no sense is it a "work of extremely high order," as Shapiro had maintained. It is "the kitchen-midden of a heart long dead: broken memories, jagged bits of spite, splinters of a distorting glass wherein the world is seen as it is not, a hodgepodge of private symbols, weary epigrams, anecdotes, resentments, chuckles, and the polyglot malapropisms that pass for erudition among the elite." Occasionally one finds "an oddment of learning" so awkwardly disguised that a sophomore can delight in identifying it, but more often the intelligible passages are confined to references to "niggers," "obscenities indicated by initials," "a tearful elegy . . . on Mussolini and his mistress," an "ironic travesty on American sentiments toward the Nazis," and many examples of "Pound's prevailing and brutal anti-Semitism." In essence the poem represents the extremes to which "cynicism and heartlessness" can go.

The absurd and dangerous error, Hillyer continues, of awarding one of the nation's highest literary awards to a man who was "arrested in Italy on a charge of treason" and who seemed "ripe for hanging" until he was judged insane and placed "under suspended indictment" is the tragic result of our turning literature over to a small group of inbred critics who insist that a work of art must be judged apart from its author and from the content of the work itself. This small coterie, called the New Critics, find the music of words repugnant and are wholly concerned "with irony, the meaning of meaning, paradoxes, ambiguities, ambivalences, dichotomies—and, indeed, any double talk." This small group of elitists have gained control of American letters because they have for their exclusive use the pages of four or five "esoteric literary reviews." As Douglas Bush suggested in "The New

Criticism: Some Old Fashioned Queries" (*PMLA*, March, 1949), reputations are made as "Mr. A quotes Mr. B, Mr. B quotes Mr. A, Mr. A and B quote Mr. C and are quoted by him." In this way, Hillyer concludes, still quoting Bush, "There emerges a picture of a little world of several dozen people who embody all the literary intelligence of the country, who form a compact and exclusive communion of saints."

The head of the dictatorial group, Hillyer believes, is T. S. Eliot, whose whole life has "been a flight from St. Louis" and who "has succeeded—where Oscar Wilde failed—in promulgating the doctrine of art-for-art's sake throughout all ranks." This small clan "has shut the doors of poetry" to all who do not belong. In addition to Eliot, whose poetry and prose "lead to an interesting dead-end and nothing more," there is Ezra Pound, who "has seldom set foot in America" and who, as Louis Untermeyer has written, is "the most belligerent expatriate of his generation." Occasionally there is an attempt to raise Allen Tate, with his small body of "stilted, adjectival pieces," to the stature of important artist. Each such effort is "frustrated at the start by the existence of his works." To his colleague John Crowe Ransom, Hillyer is not less unkind; but his comments are a little more guarded. First of all, Ransom is the editor of one of those "subsidized, esoteric little literary journals" which publish the work of Mr. A, Mr. B, and Mr. C. Moreover he is undoubtedly one of the three undistinguished gentlemen designated by letters of the alphabet above, who no longer dare to write of Eliot as Ransom had written in 1923, when he had called *The Waste Land* one of the most "insubordinate" poems in the English language. "But I do not mean," Ransom had written then, "in saying this to indicate that it is permanently a part of the language; I do not entertain that as a possibility. The genius of our language is notoriously given to feats of hospitality; but it seems to me that it will be hard pressed to find accommodations at the same time for two such incompatibles as Mr. Wordsworth and the present Mr. Eliot; and any realist must admit that what happens to be the prior tenure of the mansion in this case is likely to be stubbornly defended."[3] Hillyer suggests that if Ransom were writing

3. John Crowe Ransom, "Waste Lands," *Literary Review*, July 14, 1923, pp. 825–26.

in 1949, his attitude would be more respectful, if not worshipful, and his criticism more moderate.

Hillyer's final charge is one that he would retract six months later in the *American Mercury*. T. S. Eliot, allegedly the determining force in the selection of Pound—though as a British citizen he was not qualified to sit on the committee—was a disciple of Carl Jung. Jung was a Nazi sympathizer and was for years an intimate of Ezra Pound's. Paul Mellon, who gave the money for the Bollingen award, which was named to honor Jung's home in Switzerland, was also a great admirer of Dr. Jung. One can easily understand, Hillyer implies, why the committee was able to overlook Pound's treasonous conduct. "What is to be done?" he asks. "The 1949 Bollingen Award is a permanent disgrace and cannot be expunged. But preventive measures against a choice can be taken. The first step would seem to be for the expatriate T. S. Eliot to be dropped from the jury." In the *American Mercury* article, Hillyer withdrew the farfetched charge regarding conspiracy, but he continued to inveigh against Eliot, even though there was nothing technically wrong with Eliot's being on the committee.

This attack was answered by many, including Luther H. Evans, the librarian of Congress, who insisted that "in my many years of studying and teaching in the field of political science I came to regard a political test for art and poetry as a sign of a dictatorial, illiberal, and undemocratic approach to matters of the mind." The response to Evans' letter was written by Norman Cousins, editor of the *Saturday Review of Literature*, who proclaimed that though art should be separated from politics, politics cannot be a substitute for values. "We do not believe," he continues, "that what a poet says is necessarily of more importance than the way he says it. . . . We do not believe that poetry can convert words into maggots that eat at human dignity and still be good poetry." Even John Gould Fletcher entered the controversy, strangely enough on the side opposite to that occupied by many of his fellow contributors to *I'll Take My Stand*. (His essay in that symposium had been called fascist.) In no way, he argued, does the *Pisan Cantos* merit the Bollingen award, for it is "very bad poetry, defaced with scurrility and anti-Semitism." Attempting to follow the "New Critical doctrine" that the aesthetic effect of a poem can be separated from its "relation to men in human society—as the Fellows have suggested—is destructive to any attempt to make poetry a vital touchstone of human experience."[4] Confusing the New Critics and the Agrarians, Rossell Hope Robbins found the philosophical attitudes of T. S. Eliot a most important influence on both groups; and he insisted that the only reason the "political position of the Southern Agrarians . . . [or] that of Eliot" is tolerated is that few Americans are aware of it.

By autumn the controversy had reached Gambier, Ohio. But Ransom was spending a year as a visiting professor at Indiana University. On September 30, 1949, D. H. Lobdell, a student, published in the *Kenyon Collegian* an article under the headline "Hillyer Sets Off Poetry Powder Keg With Pound Attack." Hillyer, Lobdell asserted, may "loosen the strangle-hold on American letters held these many years by mad Ezra Pound, T. S. Eliot and other high priests of incomprehensibility worshipped by the 'New Critics.'" For years a small group of critics writing in small esoteric journals like the *Kenyon Review* have bandied "small disagreements back and forth to maintain an illusion of independent thought but in all important matters they are at one." Hillyer, the writer concludes, is likely to bring some much-needed changes not only in the literary world generally but at Kenyon and specifically in the *Kenyon Review:* "Kenyon, cathedra of John Crowe Ransom, archdeacon in Poetry's New Priesthood and home bailiwick for the ultra avant-garde *Kenyon Review*, undoubtedly is in for a series of minor tremors as critical reputations hit the dust."

As soon as the article appeared, Ransom's friends at Kenyon gathered to see what they should do: Denham Sutcliffe, chairman of the English department; Charles Coffin, Ransom's closest associate in the English department; and Philip Blair Rice, associate editor of the *Review*. It was finally decided that Sutcliffe would write Ransom to ascertain whether he was willing for them to write a joint letter to the *Collegian* in his defense. "I'm greatly touched," Ransom responded on October 5, "by your solicitude for my feelings, and your (and Phil's and Charles') defense of me while I'm *in absentia*." His best advice, however, was to ignore the whole matter. "[I] am awfully tired," he writes, "of

4. Luther Evans, "A Letter from the Library of Congress," *Saturday Review of Literature,* July 2, 1949, p. 20; "Ezra Pound and the Bollingen Award," *ibid.,* June 11, 1949.

people wondering about the *politics* of my, or anybody's, critical position. . . . That Kenyon boy was sure to crop-up. I'd have laughed at him I think." Nevertheless the matter might become troublesome, Ransom admits, because the article might show "the harm that the sailor-poet's tactics have done. He's raised up the middle-brows against the high-brows; like the woman in Yeats who 'set the little houses against the great' . . . ; and I'm afraid he'll offer a cheap currency which will drive out the dear (in the sense that his exercises will be easier than ours)." After this statement Ransom attempts to dismiss the entire affair: "But then he may be regretting his summer's madness himself for all I know."[5] Although Rice, Coffin, and Sutcliffe did not respond to the Lobdell attack, the next issue of the *Collegian* carried a letter from Gordon K. Chalmers. "If one of the purposes of Mr. Lobdell's article in Friday's *Collegian*," he begins, "was to discredit the work of a distinguished man of letters and admired member of the Kenyon faculty, John Crowe Ransom, I hope that your readers will reflect that his work is internationally held in high esteem and is one of the occasions for admiration of the College itself."

Ransom was willing to let the matter rest, but Allen Tate was of another opinion. He and John Berryman drafted a letter of protest to the *Saturday Review of Literature* and submitted it to one hundred writers for their signatures. Eventually eighty of the writers signed the letter. Conspicuously absent were the names of Wallace Stevens, who said that whatever happened in the *Saturday Review of Literature* was of no consequence and should be ignored; and Archibald MacLeish, who indicated that though he deplored Hillyer's tactics, he disagreed with the committee's decision because he thought *Pisan Cantos* was poor poetry. The statement by Tate and Berryman reads in part:

> The literary and political values of the poetry of Ezra Pound offer wide latitude of support and opposition, as all poetry does in one degree or another. Discussion of the Bollingen award in these terms was to be welcomed.
>
> But the methods employed by Robert Hillyer in the recent attacks published in your pages (June 11 and 18, 1949), and supported by

---

5. Thomas Daniel Young and George Core (eds.), *Selected Letters of John Crowe Ransom* (Baton Rouge, 1985), 343–44.

your recent editorials, are in our opinion reprehensible, in the following terms:

Under pretense of attacking the award of the Bollingen Prize to Ezra Pound, you sanctioned and guided a prepared attack on modern poetry and criticism, impugning not only the literary reputations but the personal characters of some of its foremost writers. . . .

We therefore protest against the methods of your attack, which in our opinion has violated the standards of responsible literary controversy, and thus has dealt a blow to American culture.

After refusing to sign this statement because of his lack of information, John Dos Passos prepared his own statement in which he complimented the committee for awarding the prize "to a poet who, erratic to the point of insanity, still remains one of the masters of the English prosody." He can make such a declaration, he continued, though he has "only aversion for Ezra Pound's political notions and no affection for his work." (Latecomers were given the choice of signing either the Tate-Berryman letter or the Dos Passos letter.) Rather than publish the two letters, the editors of the *Saturday Review of Literature* demanded to know the names of the writers who refused to sign them. The letters were withdrawn, and were published in the *Nation* on December 17, 1949.

The statements were sent not only to writers but also to "a selected list of English departments." When Denham Sutcliffe received a copy from Cleanth Brooks, he responded: "I wholly agree with the statements in the letter; so do some of my colleagues in this and other departments. We discussed the wisdom of our signing it, and concluded that by doing so we should conceivably do more harm to the local situation than good to the larger one." The "local situation" to which Sutcliffe referred was the investigation by the standing committee on the state of the college which concerned the circumstances surrounding the employment of Robert Hillyer. Specifically, this group was attempting to determine whether Hillyer had been employed by President Gordon K. Chalmers without his consulting Sutcliffe and other members of the English department. Presumably some members of the faculty suspected that Hillyer was brought to Kenyon to counteract the influence of Ransom and the *Kenyon Review*. After learning of the committee's activities from Philip Blair Rice, Ransom wrote Sutcliffe on January 11, 1950:

The President seems to have denied that he failed to consult with you as Chairman of English before his appointment of Hillyer. I believe I have something pertinent on that. It has to do with the original appointment which brought Hillyer to Kenyon the second semester of last year. . . . It must have been [one] morning in the fall of 1948 that the President sent for me, and said he wanted to tell me *before he told anyone else* that he had invited Hillyer, and received Hillyer's acceptance. I felt that the President was being gentle with me, or meant to be, on the ground that I might have suspected he was bringing in my rival and possible supplanter. . . .

This is stale and unpleasant stuff. . . . I have been enjoying my distance of relative peace here, and for God's sake don't imagine I'm looking for trouble. But if you need to put on record what I have just written it is there for you; or I will come and deliver it.[6]

Sutcliffe replied to Ransom on January 16 that Chalmers "believes he did consult" him about inviting Hillyer; but Sutcliffe insisted, "When I was first told anything about the matter, Hillyer had already been invited to come." When Chalmers was asked by the committee whether the members of the English department had approved Hillyer's appointment, Chalmers said that "'many people on the faculty and in the community' thought it a good thing. He *seemed* to say some members of this department thought it a good thing. He was not pressed for names, but I cannot imagine whom he had in mind." Shortly after writing this letter, Sutcliffe made an official statement to S. B. Cummings, chairman of the committee: He was not "in any effective sense" consulted about Hillyer's appointment as a part-time visiting professor. Although he and Chalmers did confer before Hillyer was given a full-time appointment in the department, they could not reach any agreement:

> My opposition [Sutcliffe wrote] sprang from Prof. Hillyer's frequently expressed opposition to our colleague, Prof. Ransom, to the Kenyon Review, and to the School of English. I objected less, perhaps, to the fact of his opposition than to the manner of it. My conviction that Professor Hillyer's presence would create disharmony was firmly established when he said to me in a letter that he was about to wage war on the "new criticism" in a book review in the *Saturday Review of Literature*. . . .

6. John Crowe Ransom to Denham Sutcliffe, January 11, 1950, in the Kenyon College Archives.

I hotly disapproved Professor Hillyer's articles in the *Saturday Review* and in the *American Mercury*. Yet when I was asked, by two different persons, to sign a letter of protest to the *Saturday Review*, I replied that I had no wish to bring the name of the College needlessly into public controversy. When a letter appeared in the Kenyon *Collegian* attacking Mr. Ransom and asserting the victory of Professor Hillyer, I dissuaded two influential colleagues from responding to that letter, and I think I helped stave off a very unpleasant incident by first going to the President and letting him see that he could save the situation. He did so.[7]

Although it seems likely that it was Ransom and Sutcliffe who dissuaded Rice and Coffin from responding to the article in the *Collegian*, it is helpful to know that Chalmers' letter in Ransom's defense was not a spontaneous reaction. Chalmers' attitude was probably most accurately expressed in a statement he made to Ransom shortly after the articles appeared in the *Saturday Review of Literature*. In a letter to Allen Tate on December 10, 1949, Ransom quotes Chalmers: "'From our discussion of the last several years with respect to the Review and the School of English, you will remember that I am necessarily concerned that the College itself as it deals with literature shall not be predominantly one thing.'"[8] The fact that Ransom had less than Chalmers' full confidence might account for the failure of the Rockefeller Foundation to continue the support of the Kenyon School of English, necessitating the move to Indiana University of one of the most prestigious programs ever sponsored by the college.

The end result of this controversy was that shortly after it developed, Hillyer resigned from Kenyon. Before his death in 1961, he published two more books of poetry, *The Relic and Other Poems* (1957) and *Collected Poems* (1961), and slipped quietly into oblivion.

The Bollingen Foundation decided to continue to award the prize with the same jury but under the auspices of Yale University. In 1949, the award was given to Wallace Stevens, and in 1950 it went to Ransom. On February 3, 1951, shortly after he had been notified of the honor, Ransom wrote Tate: "Naturally, I was 100% surprised . . . and 99% pleased of course; the small

---

7. The letters from Sutcliffe are in the Kenyon College Archives.
8. Young and Core (eds.), *Selected Letters of John Crowe Ransom*, 345.

reservation being the faint suspicion that I may have owed it in some degree to the Committee's (unconscious) idea of using Ransom as a stick to beat Hillyer and [*The Saturday Review of Literature*] with."⁹

Although Hillyer and the *Saturday Review* clearly instigated the controversy, it was symptomatic of a growing disaffection for the New Criticism. In the winter of 1949, Robert Gorham Davis charged in the *American Scholar* that for twenty years or more "*authority, hierarchy, catholicism, aristocracy, tradition, absolutes, dogma, truths*" have become "related terms of honor, and *liberalism, naturalism, scientism, individualism, equalitarianism, progress, protestantism, pragmatism,* and *personality*" have become "related terms of rejection and contempt." He had reached this conclusion, he wrote, after studying closely *I'll Take My Stand, Who Owns America?*, the criticism of Tate, Yvor Winters, and Ransom (particularly *God Without Thunder*). Convincing evidence, he continued, is everywhere apparent in the pages of the *Southern Review,* the *Sewanee Review,* the *Kenyon Review,* Eliot's *Criterion,* and the *American Review,* and most obviously in the essays of Donald Davidson, Cleanth Brooks, Tate, Yvor Winters, Austin Warren, and Ransom. Winters was infuriated by the article and responded immediately, calling the essay a disgrace to the *American Scholar* and pointing out the absurdity of assigning any one political persuasion to the many persons usually classified as New Critics. Although he believed that the Southern Agrarians were "fanaticists," few, if any, of them were fascists. Finally, he insisted that anyone confusing the southern Agrarians and the New Critics was ignorant of the most important developments in modern American thought.

As we look back on this controversy after thirty years, certain conclusions seem inevitable. The first is that no attempt was made to differentiate between the New Critics and the Southern Agrarians. Since some of the same persons were involved in the activities of both movements—particularly Ransom and Tate—it was assumed that the aims and purposes of both were identical.

9. *Ibid.,* 360. The remaining American poets on the committee—with the exception of Lowell (who won the Bollingen translation prize in 1962)—subsequently received the prize: Auden in 1954, Adams and Bogan in 1955, Aiken in 1956, Tate in 1957, and Shapiro in 1969.

(Davidson was labeled a New Critic, though he had announced in print many times that his critical persuasions were very different from those of Ransom and Tate; Brooks was made an Agrarian, though his essay in *Who Owns America?* was almost his only contribution to the movement; Austin Warren was apparently considered a Southern Agrarian, though his only connection with that group was a few visits south of his midwestern home.)

The tumult over awarding the Bollingen prize to Ezra Pound went much deeper, it would seem, than a reaction to this specific event. Giving one of the nation's most prestigious literary awards to an avowed fascist merely provided the occasion for Robert Hillyer and many other discontented literary journalists and commentators to strike out at the most important group of literary critics produced in the western world between the two great wars. Since some of the best-known persons usually classified as New Critics had once contributed to *I'll Take My Stand* (1930), it is not surprising that many of the arguments leveled at the New Critics were the same as those that had been aimed at the Agrarians fifteen years earlier. In 1936, in *Fight*, a Communist journal, Grace Lumpkin had interviewed Seward Collins, the editor of the *American Review*, the journal that in the thirties carried many articles by the Agrarians. Collins asserted that he and many of the Agrarians had the same economic aims, that he and Tate had the same religious views, and he admitted that he was a fascist. "I admire Hitler and Mussolini very much," he said, because "they have done great things for their countries." He even accepted Hitler's treatment of the Jews. "It is not persecution," he asserted; "the Jews make trouble. It is necessary to segregate them." As she ended her interview, Miss Lumpkin made an association between the ideas of Collins and those of some of the Agrarians. After reading *I'll Take My Stand, God Without Thunder*, and extensively in the *Southern Review* and the *American Review*, she was convinced that "there is the beginning of a group that is preparing the philosophical and moral" climate for the development of fascism.

When Tate read the interview, he was enraged, and he wrote Davidson on February 23, 1936, that they must break with Collins immediately. He added, however: "*American Review* is a mighty convenient place to publish things. But if we're to have everything we write discredited with charges of . . . Fascism, all we shall get out of it is the check, and I imagine we might make more money in some other business." Tate wrote Collins suggesting a lawsuit against Lumpkin; but when Collins took no action Tate wrote a letter to the *New Republic* declaring that he was "deeply opposed to fascism" and that he would choose "communism if it were the alternative."[10] Miss Lumpkin responded by quoting from essays what she considered to be incriminating evidence; and Collins' letter to the *New Republic* merely clouded the issue. Although he said he was speaking for no one except himself, he asserted that "as I have pointed out to them and as Miss Lumpkin's letter illustrates, there is too much similarity between their avowed ideas and those prevalent in fascist movements [for them] to escape being called fascists." The *New Republic* responded to this correspondence with an unsigned essay—Virginia Rock thinks it was written by Malcolm Cowley—which asserts: "Some theories of the Southern Agrarians are quite close to part of Hitler's and Mussolini's programs—the demagogic part of them naturally." A few months after this exchange, the Marxist critic V. F. Calverton called the Agrarians a dangerous group of reactionaries, and Peter Carmichael found in one of Frank L. Owsley's essays some "remarkable proposals . . . which reek [of] fascism and Nazism."

This controversy, like many other literary disagreements in the United States, progressed far beyond the simple and straightforward question that initiated it: Should a traitor be given one of the most prestigious literary awards offered by the country that he had renounced? As the controversy continued, Ezra Pound was apparently forgotten. The Agrarians were illogically and simplistically merged into the New Critics, and the bases upon which they were ridiculed and condemned shifted from their economic and political attitudes to their theories of literature.

(1980)

10. Tate correspondence can be found in the Harvey S. Firestone Memorial Library, Princeton University.

The Evolution of "Lee in the Mountains"

DONALD DAVIDSON spent the college year of 1932 to 1933 in Marshallville, Georgia, the home of his good friend John Donald Wade. For several years, Davidson, like some of his fellow Agrarians, had been intensely interested in Southern history, particularly Civil War history.[1] *I'll Take My Stand: The South and the Agrarian Tradition* had been published in 1930 and dedicated to Professor Walter Fleming, an eminent Southern historian. Although Davidson's contribution to that symposium was concerned primarily with the plight of the arts and artists in an industrial society, his interest in the developments of the twentieth century had led him to look carefully at many facets of Southern history. During the spring of 1933, at the home of Andrew Lytle's father in Guntersville, Alabama, he met several of the other contributors to *I'll Take My Stand*. At this meeting, Seward Collins, editor and publisher of the *Bookman*, discussed his plans for the *American Review* and indicated that he would welcome contributions from the Agrarians and others of their point of view.[2]

From 1933 to 1936, when the second symposium—*Who Owns*

This essay originally appeared, in slightly different form, in *Donald Davidson: An Essay and a Bibliography*, by Thomas Daniel Young and M. Thomas Inge (Nashville, 1965). Copyright © 1965 by Vanderbilt University Press. Reprinted by permission of the Vanderbilt University Press.

1. During this period, too, Davidson was reading Charles A. Beard's *The Rise of American Civilization* (1927) and F. J. Turner's *The Significance of Sections in American History* (1932), two books that figure prominently in Davidson's study of sectionalism: *The Attack on Leviathan* (Chapel Hill, 1938).

2. This meeting was a continuation of one that had occurred earlier in Nashville. Davidson said that in the Guntersville meeting the Agrarians discussed, among other topics, the means by which they could give literary emphasis to the forthcoming journal. Interview with Davidson, October 2, 1962.

America?—was published, Davidson was advancing on many fronts the primary beliefs that he continues to hold.[3] During these years he presented ordered, cogent arguments in behalf of his Agrarian principles in such divergent publications as the *Southern Review, American Review, Hound and Horn, American Mercury, Virginia Quarterly Review, Progressive Farmer,* and several Southern newspapers. While Davidson was preparing these prose essays, he was carrying a full teaching schedule at Vanderbilt University in the regular academic year and at the Bread Loaf School of English of Middlebury College during the summers. One may well wonder, therefore, how there was any time left for poetry.

But 1932 to 1933 was a year of relative leisure. He was free of his teaching and, though he was engaged in correspondence with Collins and his fellow Agrarians, planning for their future association with *American Review;* there was time for reading and writing. He read widely in American history and wrote "Old Black Joe," "Randall, My Son," and "The Running of Streight," three poems that were later to appear in *Lee in the Mountains and Other Poems.* During the winter of 1932 and the early spring of 1933, he composed his essay "Sectionalism in the United States," which appeared in the July–September issue of *Hound and Horn.* Apparently the idea for a poem on Lee had been in his mind for some time and his reading in Southern history and his serious considerations of Southern problems undoubtedly pushed these half-formed concepts to a prominent position in his creative consciousness. When he left Georgia in the late spring for his teaching assignment at Bread Loaf, the idea for the poem was beginning to take shape. In late August he committed to paper a draft of a poem which at that time was called "General Lee Remembers." This first written draft, which contains only 61 lines, differs in many essential respects from the final version of 121 lines completed in January, 1934, and read later in the same month in Nashville at a United Daughters of the Confederacy luncheon. Starting with this first draft in August, 1933, and including the final one in January of the next year, Davidson wrote five versions of the poem that is now "Lee in the Mountains." All of them exist in manuscript, and a close reading of them not only shows the evolution of Davidson's best-known poem but

---

3. This essay was written in 1964.

also furnishes a concrete example of some of the specific ways a work by one of the Fugitives was affected by the frank criticism of another member of the group. When Davidson had completed the fourth draft of the poem—what he apparently thought was the final version—he sent it to Allen Tate for comment. At Benfolly, Tate's home near Clarksville, Tennessee, Tate and his wife, Caroline Gordon, read the poem; Tate's letter of January 19, three days after he had received the poem, and his comments in the margins of the manuscript indicate the reactions of these two close friends of Davidson's.

Davidson has described the manner in which a typical Fugitive meeting was conducted,[4] and many critics have commented upon the unique nature of the communal efforts of this group. Some have expressed the belief that the renaissance in Southern literature would not have occurred "without the vigorous movement in criticism which preceded it,"[5] and the work of the Fugitive group has been cited as the outstanding example of the values that accrue when a group of poet-critics discuss in detail each other's poetry.[6] Although the values of this procedure are generally recognized, no one has provided an actual example of the process at work. Davidson's revision of "Lee in the Mountains" in the light of Tate's comments demonstrates how one Fugitive poet was able to incorporate into his work some of the suggestions offered by his fellow poet and critic.

Here is Davidson's description of a typical Fugitive meeting:

> First we gave strict attention, from the beginning, to the *form* of poetry. The very nature of our meeting facilitated and intensified such attention, and probably influenced Fugitive habits of composition. Every poem was read aloud by the poet himself, while the members of the group had before them typed copies of the poem. The reading aloud might be followed by a murmur of compliments, but often enough there was a period of ruminative silence before anyone said a word. Then discussion began, and it was likely to be ruthless in its exposure on any technical weakness as to rhyme, meter, imagery, metaphor and was often minute in analysis of details. . . .
>
> This process of intensive criticism, characteristic of the Fugitive

---

4. Donald Davidson, *Southern Writers in the Modern World* (Athens, Ga., 1958), 21–22.

5. Richmond Croom Beatty, Floyd C. Watkins, and Thomas Daniel Young (eds.), *The Literature of the South* (Chicago, 1952), 613.

6. Louise Cowan, *The Fugitive Group* (Baton Rouge, 1959), xix.

meetings, carried over into private conversation between meetings when we could discuss our poems more informally. It was still more highly developed in the correspondence and exchange of manuscripts when this or that member was absent from Nashville. I will venture to say that this latter type of criticism was more beneficial, because it allowed deliberation. The most helpful criticism I ever received—and the sternest—was from Allen Tate, in the marginal notations on manuscripts that I sent him and in the very frank letters that always came with the return of a manuscript.[7]

In the letter to Tate dated January 15, 1934, which was included in the package containing the "Lee in the Mountains" manuscript, Davidson remarks: "I am painfully aware that my conception far outruns my execution in this poem. I am not in the least satisfied with it." The poem at this time had gone through four complete versions and was yet to be considerably revised before it was published for the first time in the May, 1934, issue of the *American Review,* but, as Davidson's remarks imply, his original conception prevailed throughout, and it was only in the strengthening and enlargement of the execution that there was revision. The first draft is only half the finished product and only eight lines of the original effort appear unchanged in the published version. It is obvious, however, that before he first put pen to paper the poet had clearly in mind the poem he would finally write. When Davidson stopped abruptly after sixty-one lines, he had presented, though in different language and a somewhat different tone, the material that appears in the first eighty lines of the completed poem.

The subject matter of the poem, covering the period between 1865 and 1870 while Lee was president of Washington College, may be divided into five parts, all presented through Lee's stream of consciousness. In Part One (ll. 1–17), as he walks across the campus toward his office, Lee is greeted by a group of students who are seated on the steps waiting for the bell to announce the daily chapel and the beginning of another day's activities. In Part Two (ll. 18–52), Lee goes into his office and resumes the labor that consumed most of his free time during these years, a revision of his father's memoirs. In Part Three (ll. 53–80), Lee ponders a question to which he must have given much attention during this crucial period of his life: Instead of attempting to justify

---

7. Davidson, *Southern Writers in the Modern World,* 2n.

his father's actions during and after the Revolutionary War, why is he not concentrating on his own experiences as leader of the military forces of the Confederacy? In Part Four (ll. 81–103), he gives the reasons for his choice and explores his present situation. In Part Five (ll. 104–121), after Lee's reminiscence is interrupted by the bell calling him to chapel, President Lee presents in essence the remarks he must have given almost daily to the students who looked to him for inspiration and leadership.[8]

The first draft of the poem, "General Lee Remembers," presents almost all of the material included in the first three parts of the completed poem.

[Draft One]

GENERAL LEE REMEMBERS

    into   shadows
Walking ~~under~~ the ~~elms~~, walking alone   1

        the   locusts
From the hitching-rack under / shadow of ~~elms~~   2

Up to the President's office. Hearing the voices   3

Whispering, *Hush, it is General Lee.* ~~Boys,~~   4

~~Take off your hats to General Lee.~~

And the soldiers' faces under the gleam of flags   5

Lifting no more on any road or field   6

    is
Where ~~still~~ Virginia still, though lost and gone   7

        perished, remembering
Sunken, and lost, and ~~tired, waiting the~~ bugles.   8

---

8. Lawrence Bowling, "An Analysis of Davidson's 'Lee in the Mountains,'" *Georgia Review*, VI (Spring, 1952), 69–88.

| It is not General Lee | Walking the rocky path; and the columns old | 9 |

                                        stones
Where the paint cracks and the grass grows in the plank   10

It is Robert   civilian who walks.
And General Lee in his dark / suit is walking   11

Under the
Lost in ~~In~~ the shadow of elms where no flag flies   12

                      his
My father's house is taken and ~~the~~ hearth   13

~~Cold as a sword that~~

Left to the candle-drippings, sown with ashes   14

Moveless as are the dreams, no more renewed   15

I cannot remember my father's hand, I cannot   16

~~Speak to~~
Answer his voice as he calls from the misty   17

Mounting where riders gather at gates,   18

~~And day break comes too far away.~~

                then
~~And~~ He was old/, I knew him not, His hand   19

Was stretched for
~~Put down to~~ mine, at daybreak snatched away   20

As he rode out and came no more. The grave   21

Lies in a far land and keeps the vow   22

I made there, once, in better days, yet knew   23

The savor of my fortune even then   24

As a man beholds with certain eyes, the drift   25

Of time, and tongues of men, and a sacred cause.   26

The fortune of the Lees is with the land   27

My father's land, which once I left. My mother   28

Knew this well, and sat among the candles   29

Reading the *Memoirs,* now so long unread   30

These faces and these voices and his hand,   31

Gone from the dream—they are Virginia still   32

The pen marches, the pages grow, the South   33

Knew my father and yet again will know   34

Ah, but to tell the tale. What's history   35

Now but a wraith clutched out of the mist,   36

                  a
Where voices are loud and ~~the~~ glut of little souls   37

In all the too much blood and the perished battles   38

What I will do is only a son's devoir   39

To a lost father, to my mother's husband   40

The rest must stay unsaid and lips be locked   41

If it were said—   42

The rivers now run clear in Virginia's Valley   43

General Lee Remembers

Walking into the shadows, walking alone
From the hitching-rack under the shadow of locusts –
Up to the President's office. Hearing the voices
Whispering, Hush, it is General Lee.
And the soldiers' faces under the gleam of flags
Lifting, no more on any road or field
Where is Virginia still, Though lost and gone
Sunken, and lost, and perished, remembering bugles.
Walking the rocky path; and the columns old
Where the paint cracks and the grass grows in the stones of the plaster
It is Robert Lee in his dark suit who awakes.
Lost in the shadow of elms where no flag flies

My father's house is taken and his hearth
Left to the candle-droppings, sown with ashes
Moveless as are the dreams, no more renewed

I cannot remember my father's hand. I cannot
Answer his voice as he calls from the misty
Mounting where riders gather at gates.
He was old then, I knew him not. His hand
was stretched for mine, at daybreak snatched away
As he rode out and came no more. The grave
Lies in a far land and keeps the vow
I made there, once, in better days, yet renew
The savor of my fortune even then
As a man beholds with certain eye, the drift
Of time, and tongues of men, and a sacred cause.
The fortune of the Lees is with the land

The first twenty-seven lines of Draft One of "Lee in the Mountains"

Clear of blood and the weeping of old women	44
Rises no more. The waves of grain begin	45
The Shenandoah is golden with new grain	46
The Blue Ridge, lapped in a haze of light	47
Harbors no war, and is at peace. The columns	48
is Pass no more; the horse ~~stands~~ at plough; the rifle	49
Returns to the chimney crotch and the hunter's hand	50
This is the peace of bondage, and I wait	51
locusts With words unsaid, thus in the shadow of ~~elms.~~	52
If it were said, and the word should run like fire	53
Like living fire into the roots of grass	54
And the sunken flag should kindle like a flame	55
And the stubborn hearts should waken, and the dream	56
Stir like a crippled phantom under the pines	57
And all the slow earth quicken into shouting	58
Above the feet of gathering men, the sword	59
Unsheathed would rush against the ranks	60
Of blue that shepherd us, that bend us into bondage.	61

 After Davidson had completed these sixty-one lines, he had to put the poem aside to return to Nashville for the opening of the fall quarter at Vanderbilt. His duties there must have consumed most of his time for several weeks, so that he probably was able to do little work on the poem until late October or early November. When he could resume his creative labor, it seems, he reworked carefully the portion already composed before attempting to complete the poem. A close examination of the appropriate sections of the second draft shows how carefully the poet worked through the first draft before attempting to finish his poem. The first important change occurs in the title. After writing "General Lee," with the apparent intention of retaining the previous title "General Lee Remembers," he crosses out both words, and the title becomes "Lee in the Mountains."

Most of the alterations in the lines of Draft One are relatively minor. Twenty lines go into the second draft without change: 1, 3, 7, 13, 14, 16, 21, 29, 30, 33, 36, 37, 41, 45, 46, 47, 50, 53, 54, and 58. Sixteen lines are unchanged except for the substitution of one or two words. For example, "And the soldiers' faces under the gleam of flags" becomes "But the soldiers' faces under the gleam of flags." Several other examples indicate the care with which the poet worked with each of the sixty-one lines of Draft One before allowing it to become a part of the revised version:

(Draft 1) Lifting no more on any road or field   Line 6
(Draft 2) Lift no more on any road or field

(1) Walking the rocky path; and the columns old   9
(2) Walking the rocky path, and the stairs are old

(1) Answer his voice as he calls from the misty   17
(2) Answer his voice as he calls far-off in the misty

(1) He was old then, I knew him not, His hand   19
(2) He was old then—I was a child—his hand

(1) Was stretched for mine, at daybreak snatched away   20
(2) Stretched for mine, some faint dawn snatched away

(1) As he rode out and came no more. The grave   21
(2) And he rode out and came no more. The grave

(1) Lies in a far land and keeps the vow   22
(2) Of Henry Lee in a far land still keeps

(1) I made there, once, in better days, yet knew   23
(2) The vow I made in better days, nor knew

The Evolution of "Lee in the Mountains" 117

(1) The fortune of the Lees is with the land 27
(2) The fortune of the Lees goes with the land

(1) Knew my father and yet again will know 34
(2) Knew my father once and again will know

(1) Ah, but to tell the tale. What's history 35
(2) Ah, but to tell the tale. What is history

(1) With words unsaid, thus in the shadow of locusts 52
(2) With words unsaid, thus in the shadow of doom

(1) Stir like a crippled phantom under the pines 57
(2) Stir like an avenging phantom under the pines

In six other lines the basic idea expressed in Draft One is given sharper focus by a change of phrasing:

(1) Sunken and lost and perished, remembering bugles 8
(2) Sunken and spent, remembering only the bugles

(1) Lost in the shadow of elms where no flag flies 12
(2) Bound in the shadow of doom where no flag flies

(1) Moveless as are the dreams, no more renewed 15
(2) Sifted and tossed like dreams that now are cold

(1) As a man beholds with certain eyes, the drift 25
    Of time, and tongues of men, and a sacred cause
(2)   God too late
    Unseals to certain eyes the drift
    Of time, and the tongues of men, and a sacred cause.

(1) The Blue Ridge, lapped in a haze of light 47
    Harbors no war, and is at peace. . . .
(2) The Blue Ridge, lapped in a haze of light,
    Thunders no more. . . .

(1) This is the peace of bondage, and I wait 51
    With words unsaid, thus in the shadow of locusts.
(2) To keep this peace of bondage and to wait
    With words unsaid, thus in the shadow of doom.

Draft Two runs to 130 lines and includes all the content of the published version of the poem. In addition, this draft contains 27 lines that appear without change in the published poem. Nine lines longer than the final version, the second draft contains some material that will subsequently be dropped and several extensive revisions that demonstrate the poet's attempts to evoke the desired response from the reader. Near the beginning of both versions, Davidson strives to establish Lee's relationship with the students of Washington College, the devotion and love that these young men must have felt for their revered leader. In Draft One, the poet wrote:

> Hearing the voices
> Whispering, *Hush, it is General Lee.* Boys
> Take off your hats to General Lee.

Obviously dissatisfied with this statement, he deleted the sentence *"Boys / Take off your hats to General Lee"* and moved on without trying to recast it. In his revision, however, he returned to the same point and wrote:

> Hearing the voices
> Whisper, *Hush it is General Lee.* The boys
> Tip their hats to General Lee.

Still not pleased, he crossed out "The boys / Tip their hats to General Lee" and wrote "Young men, / Receive the loneliness of this salute to you." Although he allowed this version to stand temporarily, the passage was considerably revised in subsequent drafts of the poem.

A little later in the poem, Davidson is trying to suggest the disparate elements competing for Lee's consciousness—his family associations and his experiences in the Civil War. In the first draft Davidson wrote:

> My mother
> Knew this well, and sat among the candles
> Reading the *Memoirs*, now so long unread
> These faces and these voices and his hand
> Gone from the dream—they are Virginia still
> The pen marches, the pages grow.

In the second draft, the poet attempts to present this conflict more concretely by indicating specific elements:

> My mother
> Knew this well and sat among the candles
> Reading the *Memoirs*, now so long unread.
> Her voice, his hand, the flags, the soldiers faces

The Evolution of "Lee in the Mountains"

>A dream's gone desire—these are Virginia still
>The pen marches, the pages grow.

This crucial passage will be considerably worked over in each of the later revisions before the poet finds the imagery to blend these two important groups of experiences.

A comparison of two other brief passages points up how Davidson succeeds in communicating Lee's reflections more vividly and concretely. The South is now at peace, and surely one would choose this scene in which "clear waters run in Virginia's Valley," rather than the slaughters of war that fill the rivers with blood and the house with "the weeping of young women."

>[DRAFT ONE]
>
>If it were said—
>The rivers now run clear in Virginia's Valley
>Clear of blood and the weeping of old women
>Rises no more. The waves of grain begin
>The Shenandoah is golden with new grain
>The Blue Ridge, lapped in a haze of light
>Harbors no war, and is at peace.

>[DRAFT TWO]
>
>If it were said, as it cannot be said
>I see clear waters run in Virginia's Valley,
>And in the house the weeping of young women
>Rises no more. The waves of grain begin.
>The Shenandoah is golden with new grain
>The Blue Ridge, lapped in a haze of light,
>Thunders no more.

The imagery of the revised passage is more effective because it is more restrained (there are no rivers of blood) and yet it is more dramatic: Now it is *young*, not *old*, women who are no longer weeping; the rather trite statement "The Blue Ridge . . . / Harbors no war" becomes more suggestively "The Blue Ridge . . . / Thunders no more."

Davidson concludes his first draft with Lee's considering what might have happened if he had chosen another course of action, if he had decided—or if he were yet to decide—to issue a call to arms. (Such a call might have seemed justifiable because of the general belief that the victor had violated the terms of the agreement at Appomattox.) In its first form the passage that indicated the reaction of the former soldiers to an expression of dissatisfaction from Lee was:

> If it were said, and the word should run like fire
> Like living fire into the roots of grass
> And the sunken flag should kindle like a flame
> And the stubborn hearts should waken, and the dream
> Stir like a crippled phantom under the pines
> And all the slow earth quicken into shouting
> Above the feet of gathering men, the sword
> Unsheathed would rush against the ranks
> Of blue that shepherd us, that bend us into bondage.

In Draft Two this passage is considerably revised:

> If it were said and the word should run like fire
> Like living fire into the roots of grass,
> The sunken flag would kindle on the hills
> The stubborn hearts would waken, and the dream
> Stir like an avenging phantom under the pines
> And all the slow earth quicken into shouting
> Beneath the feet of gathering men—the sword
> Locks in the sheath. The sword of Lee
> Bows to the rust that cankers, and the guns
> Mouldering keep the forlorn peace of bondage.

In the revised form the results of Lee's decision to call again upon his former soldiers are positively and decisively stated: "The sunken flag would kindle" and "the stubborn hearts would waken" (note the change from the conditional "should" of Draft One); "the dream / [would] Stir like an avenging phantom" (in the first version it was a "crippled phantom"). But here Lee retreats quickly before the almost certain repercussion of this decision, a reaction much nearer that of Lee in the published poem. In the first draft "the sword / Unsheathed would rush against the ranks / Of blue that shepherd us, that bend us into bondage." But now President Lee in the quietness of his study, almost as quickly as the thought flashes across his consciousness, realizes he cannot entertain the thought of resuming the war. Despite the obvious provocation, what he must do is clear. "The sword of Lee / Bows to the rust that cankers, and the guns / Mouldering keep the forlorn peace of bondage."

With the resolution of this crux, the poet moves on to complete the poem. Now that Lee has made his choice, he continues his anguished examination of his present situation.

> Among these boys, whose eyes lift up to mine
> Within these walls where droning wasps repeat
> A sinister reveille, I still must face
> The grim flag-bearer thundering with his summons
> Once more to surrender, now to surrender all.

Among the most unpleasant of his memories is his recollection that he foresaw the disastrous conclusion of the war before the others did and strongly suspects he could have altered its course.[9]

> The mountains, once I said, in the little room
> At Richmond, by the huddled fire, and still
> The President shook his head. The mountains wait,
> I said, in the long beat and rattle of siege, and the thunder
> Of cratered Petersburg. Too late, too late,
> We sought the mountains, and those people came.

So he is "in the mountains now beyond Appomattox / Listening long for voices that will not speak / Again." At this point the poet has difficulty rendering the specific details that his memory recalls. First he writes:

> waiting the rapid hoofs of the courier a rider
> To lift the flap and enter. Is it the plume
> Of Stuart? Is it the form of Hill? A. P. Hill
> The red beard
> The rough step of Early.

But this passage is deleted and he writes:

> hearing the hoofbeats come and go and fade
> Without a stop, without a brown hand lifting
> The tent-flap, under the shadow of locusts,

---

9. That Lee seriously considered taking his army to the mountains and continuing the war from there is indicated by a statement made by Jefferson Davis at a memorial service for General Lee, November 3, 1870, and reported in the Richmond *Dispatch*, November 4, 1870: "When in the last campaign he was beleaguered at Petersburg, and painfully aware of the straits to which we were reduced, he said, 'With my army in the mountains of Virginia I could carry on this war for twenty years longer.' . . . In surrender he anticipated conditions that have not been fulfilled." (Quoted by Hudson Strode in *Jefferson Davis: The Tragic Hero: The Last Twenty-five Years, 1864–1889* [New York, 1964], 370.)

> Nor even on the long white road the flag
> Of Jackson's quick brigades or the eyes of Hill
> Flashing through dust and musketry or Stuart
> Laughing beneath his plume.

Even in its revised form most of this passage will be dropped in the next draft of the poem, as will the one that follows:

> I am alone
> Trapped, consenting, taken, at last in the mountains.
> My people, we must wait—it is useless now
> To rise against the Myrmidons. Tall Troy is fallen
> So let us wait and waiting hush the murmur
> Of bitter cries until our time is come.

At this point the meditations are interrupted by the bell calling him to chapel, and Draft Two ends, as the succeeding ones will, with the presentation of Lee's remarks before the students in chapel, an affirmation of faith in a just and merciful God who will never forsake "His children and his children's children forever / To all generations of the faithful heart. Amen."

There is apparently no way to determine exactly the amount of time that elapsed between the completion of the second and third drafts of the poem. Davidson recalls that he devoted a major portion of the time he could allow for creative activity during the fall and early winter of 1933 to the writing and rewriting of this poem. Since he did not complete the first draft until early September, did not begin the second draft until the first or second week in October, and finished two more completely revised versions of the poem before he wrote Tate on January 15, 1934—the diligence with which he pursued his task is most evident.[10]

Draft Three contains 118 lines and includes 22 lines, in addition to the 8 of Draft One and the 30 of Draft Two, that appear unchanged in the first published version of the poem. After two thorough rewritings of his first attempt, then, the poet has written 60 lines—almost half the completed poem—with which he will remain satisfied through the two remaining revisions.

Again, a detailed comparison of Draft Two and Draft Three

---

10. Davidson says on this point, "I may have been under pressure from Allen Tate to finish a poem for the forthcoming 'Poetry number' of the *American Review*. I can't remember all this with absolute clearness, but am sure a poem was wanted by me."

is enlightening in tracing the development of the poem. Draft Two is important because in it the poet first gets down on paper the essential content of his poem, and Draft Three reveals the painstaking efforts of the artist as he attempts to mould his material into its final form. Davidson's revisions of Draft Two are not predominantly concerned with word changes and changes within lines. These are yet to come. (Fifty-seven lines are carried forward without change. In 21 others there is the substituting of but one or two words.) The alterations that do occur, however, are significant. In some instances, the poet is apparently attempting to make the poetic experience more vivid and accessible. Examples of this sort are many. "Bound in the shadow of doom where no flag flies" becomes "Commanding in a dream where no flag flies." "Left to the candle-drippings, sown with ashes / Sifted and tossed like dreams that now are cold" is changed to "Left to the candle-drippings where the ashes / Whirl as the chimney breathes on the cold stone."

Some of the changes are apparently an effort to enhance the sensuous quality of the verse. In line 30, for example, "Reading the *Memoirs*" becomes "Fingering the *Memoirs*." The passage beginning at line 36 has been altered for a similar purpose. In Draft Two, it reads:

> Ah, but to tell the tale. What is history
> Now but a wraith and a clutching out of the mist
> Where voices are loud and a glut of little souls
> Laps at the too much blood and the perished battles.

In Draft Three, this passage is significantly altered by the insertion of a simple question, the rearrangement of the word order, and the substitution of a few words.

> Why did my father write? Did he foresee
> History clutched as a wraith in blowing mist
> Where voices are loud, and a glut of little souls
> Laps at the too much blood and the perished battles.

Perhaps the best example of the revision of the loose, abstractly phrased exclamation to the sharp imagistic presentation found in good poetry may be seen in the two versions of the passage beginning at line 41:

> They will have their say, and I shall not have mine
> But with my father's pen that wrote in vain

> Of old neglected forays and lost triumphs
> I write, in vain, and tell what can be told
> The rest must go unsaid, and the lips be locked.

In Draft Three it is expanded to read:

> He had his say, then—I shall not have mine
> What I must do is only a son's devoir
> To a long-lost father—let him speak for me
> The rest must pass to men who never knew
> The grim and sure out-reach of moving armies
> Or heard the keen Confederate battle-cry
> Behind the spinning smoke or saw the tense
> Eyes of Virginia boys encounter death.
> I write—in vain—I tell what can be told
> The rest must go unsaid and the lips be locked.

As one would suspect, not all attempts of this kind were so successful as this one—and even this passage will be further refined in Draft Four. The five-line passage beginning at line 55 of Draft Two, though considerably altered in Draft Three, does not appear in Draft Four. The Draft Two version goes as follows:

> There is no war, and yet there is no peace.
> I gave my word and was betrayed
> And did I thus betray? And did I vow
> To keep the peace of bondage and to wait
> With words unsaid, thus in the shadow of doom.

In Draft Three it reads:

> But still the raven tears my heart? Is this
> The peace to which I bowed my head. It is
> A peace of bondage grinding me to wait
> With words unsaid, here in the shadow of doom.

It is revealing also to note the parts of Draft Two that are omitted from Draft Three. There are three rather conspicuous omissions: lines 75–79, 92–97, and 108–111.

> This is the last Gethsemane of men who love
> A land and people close as a mother's breast
> I had rather die a thousand deaths, but cannot
> Die as a soldier dies. In the crumpled paper,
> The scratching paper and the blotter of memory

> But Lee is in the mountains now, in Virginia mountains
> And all that I thought or dreamed of once is done
> If I had known what now I know, when day
> Breaks with a silent message and no thunder
> Of guns, no bugle call, no tramp of men
> I would not go to this surrender armless, so,
>
> My people, we must wait—it is useless now
> To rise against the Myrmidons. Tall Troy is fallen
> So let us wait and waiting hush the murmur
> Of bitter cries until our time is come

The deletion of these lines is not the result of the poet's changing his mind about what he wants to say. On the contrary, they state an important aspect of the theme, but too boldly, too directly. In subsequent revisions the poet will express by indirection, will suggest, the sentiment and feeling borne in these lines. Lee's belief that he has been betrayed, that his former enemy has not fulfilled the just and humane terms of surrender, is an important part of the poem. So, too, are Lee's fears that he might have failed to justify the trust placed in him by his followers. In the years between 1865 and 1870, the poet is saying, Lee must have realized that the terms offered at Appomattox were unrealistic. He has been misled by his own sense of honesty and justice. Should he have withdrawn to the mountains and made the enemy seek him out? Small bands of guerrilla warriors could have prolonged the war almost endlessly; perhaps the enemy could have been plagued and molested until his desire for peace was genuine. Understanding of Lee's doubts and questions is preliminary to an understanding of his attitude during the period covered in the poem. But the poet realizes that his mode of expression is wrong. The conflict is so boldly stated that the credible personality of Lee is in danger of being destroyed. The poet is too much involved personally, and this involvement encroaches upon the point of view he has adopted for the poem. The illusion of reality is stronger without these lines than with them; the poetic experience is not disrupted. The reader must share Lee's agonized struggles and not consider with Davidson his opinion of what the situation probably was. The less direct, more suggestive manner in which this basic conflict is presented in the published version of the poem accomplishes this objective completely.

After making the extensive revisions that went into Draft Three, Davidson was well enough satisfied with the poem to prepare a typewritten manuscript to send to Allen Tate for his comments. The search to find the exact manner of expressing the poet's conception of Lee's character continues, apparently, even during the actual typewriting. Although sixty-three lines of Draft Three go unchanged into Draft Four, the never-ending process of refinement goes on. There are numerous examples of the poet's attempt to make his references more specific and meaningful: "my hearth" becomes "his hearth" (14); "And all the torn earth" is changed to "And this torn earth" (73); "the land" to "this land" (27); and "On these green altars" to "On your altars" (105). There are examples, too, of the poet's substituting an evocative connotative word for one less suggestive: "stubborn hearts" becomes "brooding hearts" (71); "avenging phantom," "crippled phantom" (72);[11] "gathering men," "ragged men" (74). Davidson's acute sensitivity to the musical quality of the line, a dominant trait in all of his best poetry, is undoubtedly responsible for the shift of word order in lines 111 and 112. The lines that appear in Draft Three as "And the fierce undying faith / And the quenchless love" are simply and effectively rearranged to read "And the fierce faith undying / And the love quenchless."

Many of the emendations are the result of the poet's efforts to substitute an image for the simple statement or to sharpen, to make more concrete and specific, the existing image. Thus, "Where the sun breaks through a ruined shadow of locusts" becomes "Where the sun falls through the ruined boughs of locusts" (2); "For the soldiers' faces under the gleam of flags" is changed to "But the soldiers' faces under the tossing flags" (5); "Where paint cracks and grass grows in the stone" is changed to "And paint cracks and grass eats on the stone" (9); "An outlaw in his own land, a voice / Commanding in a dream where no flag flies" becomes "An outlaw fumbling for the latch, a voice / Commanding in a dream where no flag flies" (12–13). This last emendation is particularly important because the poet has found an image that suggests Lee's predicament and sets the tone for his opening section. Lee is in fact an outlaw; and, at this point, he is actually "fumbling for the latch" that will open the door to

---

11. He had written "crippled phantom" in the first draft.

his office; so the lines take the reader with Lee as he crosses the campus and reaches his office door (after he opens the door and enters the office, the second section of the poem begins—his meditations as he resumes work on his father's memoirs). But the phrase suggests, more significantly, the fundamental conflict of the poem: How is Lee, a man without official power or position, to assist the thousands of people—the students at Washington College and the residents of the South generally—who are looking to him for leadership in these "Black Raven Days of Reconstruction"? What course of action can he or should he take?

An examination of the alterations of the passage beginning at line 81 reveals the poet's endeavoring to rid his poem of excess verbiage and to make his projection of Lee's dilemma more graphic. In Draft Three, this passage is:

> I face what once I saw, before others knew,
> A phantom rising where the flags reeled down
> Within the smoke of Gettysburg or the tangled
> Cry of the Wilderness wounded, bloody with doom,
> The cold and last solution of all striving.

The revised form is more effective:

> Without arms or men I stand, but with bitter knowledge
> I face what long I saw, before others knew
> When Pickett's men streamed back and I heard the tangled
> Cry of the Wilderness wounded, bloody with doom.

On January 15, 1934, when Davidson had completed Draft Four, the first typewritten manuscript of his poem, he sent a copy to Allen Tate, and it was this copy that Tate and Caroline Gordon read at Benfolly. In his accompanying letter, Davidson called his poem "a tentative draft"—despite the fact that it had undergone many revisions and had been completely rewritten three times—and indicated his dissatisfaction with its present state. "I am not in the least satisfied with it," he wrote; "I don't know whether it will ever do. But I want you to see the poem."[12]

Apparently Tate read the poem immediately, for he returned it on January 19, 1934, and, along with the marginal comments, he sent a rather long letter, excerpted below:

12. Donald Davidson to Allen Tate, January 15, 1934, in the Harvey S. Firestone Memorial Library, Princeton University.

Your Lee poem is the finest you have ever written. I say this deliberately after much meditation and study of it. I thought your other recent poems, in the last couple of years, too argumentative and documentary. This new one is about Lee and about a great deal more than Lee. It is a very fine poem. If you lose what you've got here and relapse into documentation, I shall come over and cut your ears off![13]

[Draft Four]

LEE IN THE MOUNTAINS
1865–1870

Walking into the shadows, walking alone	1
Where the sun falls through the ruined boughs of locusts,	2
Up to the president's office.[a] Hearing the voices	3
Whisper, *Hush it is General Lee!*	4
But the soldier's faces under the tossing flags	5
Lift no more by any road or field,	6
And I am spent with battle and old[b] sorrow.	7
Walking the rocky path, where the steps decay	8
And the paint cracks and grass eats on the stone.	9
It is not General Lee, young men . . .	10
It is Robert Lee in a dark civilian suit who walks,	11

13. Allen Tate to Donald Davidson, January 19, 1934, *ibid.*
[a] Tate indicates that a paragraph division should come here and points out "a little abrupt as it is punctuated." His other comments, written in the margins of Draft Four, will be given in footnotes; the places at which they occur in the text will be indicated by superscript letters.
[b] "More definite?"

An outlaw fumbling for the latch, a voice   12

Commanding in a dream where no flag flies.[c]   13

My father's house is taken and his hearth   14

Left to the candle-drippings where the ashes   15

Whirl at a chimney-breath on the cold stone.   16

I can hardly remember my father's look, I cannot   17

Answer his voice as he calls farewell in the misty   18

Mounting where riders gather at gates.   19

He was old then—I was a child—his hand   20

Held out for mine, some daybreak snatched away,   21

And he rode out, a beaten man. Now let   22

          surer
His lone grave keep, ~~deeper~~ than cypress roots   23

The vow I made beside him. God too late   24

Unseals to certain eyes the drift   25

Of time and the hopes of men and a sacred cause.   26

The fortune of the Lees goes with this land   27

Whose sons can keep it still. My mother   28

Told me much. She sat among the candles,   29

Fingering the *Memoirs*, now so long unread,   30

[c]"See letter" [Tate is referring to his letter to Davidson, previously cited.]

And as my pen moves on across the page	31
Her voice comes back, a filmy[d] distillation	32
Of old Virginia splendors[e] done to death,	33
The hurt of all that was and cannot be.	34
Why did my father write? I know he saw	35
History clutched as a wraith out of blowing mist	36
Where voices are loud, and a glut of little souls	37
Laps at the too much blood and the burning house.	38
He would have his say, but I shall not have mine.	39
What I do is only a son's devoir	40
To a lost father. Let him only speak.	41
The rest must pass to men who never knew	42
(But on a written page) the strike of armies,	43
And never heard the long Confederate war-cry[f]	44
Charge through the muzzling smoke or saw the bright	45
Eyes of the beardless boys go up to death.[g]	46
It is Robert Lee who writes with his father's hand—	47
The rest must go unsaid and the lips be locked.	48

[d] "omit adjective?"
[e] "Is this word in character?"
[f] Tate encircles "war" and notes "Read line without this. Isn't it better?"
[g] Tate places parentheses around lines 45 and 46 and exclaims "Fine!"

If all were told, as it cannot be told— 49

If all the dread opinion of the heart 50

Now could speak, now in the shame and torment 51

Lashing the bound and trampled States— 52

If a word were said, as it cannot be said— 53

I see clear waters run in Virginia's Valleys, 54

And in the house the weeping of young women 55

Rises no more. The waves of grain begin. 56

The Shenandoah is golden with new grain. 57

The Blue Ridge, lapped in a haze of light, 58

Thunders no more. The horse is at plough. The rifle 59

Returns to the chimney crotch and the hunter's hand. 60

And nothing else than this? Was it for this 61

That on an April day we stacked ~~the~~ our arms 62

Obedient to a soldier's trust—to sink, to lie 63

Ground by the vaunting heels of little men, 64

Forever maimed, defeated, lost, impugned? 65

And was I then betrayed? Did I betray? 66

If it were said, as still it might be said— 67

If it were said, and a word should run like fire, 68

Like living fire into the roots of grass,	69
The sunken flag would kindle on wild hills,	70
The brooding hearts would waken, and the dream	71
Stir like a crippled phantom under the pines,	72
And this torn earth would quicken into shouting	73
Beneath the feet of ragged men—	74
The sword	
Locks in its sheath, the sword of Robert Lee	75
Bows to the rust that cankers and the silence.[h]	76
Among these boys whose eyes lift up to mine	77
Within gray walls where droning wasps repeat	78
A fumbling reveille, I still must face	79
Day after day, the courier with his summons	80
Once more to surrender, now to surrender all.	81
Without arms or men I stand, but with bitter knowledge[i]	82
I face what long I saw, before others knew	83
When Pickett's men streamed back and I heard the tangled	84

[h] Tate places parentheses around lines 75 and 76 and comments, "Sword too conventional. Not dramatic, but oratorical and I think out of Lee's psychology. Preceding lines so good they deserve better than this."

[i] Tate encircles "bitter" and places a question mark above it. After "knowledge" he writes in "only." Apparently he is recommending that this line read, "Without arms or men I stand, but with knowledge only."

Cry of the Wilderness wounded, bloody with doom.

The mountains, once I said, in the little room

At Richmond, by the huddled fire, but still

The President shook his head. The mountains wait,

I said in the long beat and rattle of siege

At cratered Petersburg. Too late

We sought the mountains and those people came.

And Lee is in mountains now, beyond Appomattox,

Listening long for voices that never will speak

Again; hearing the hoofbeats come and go and fade

Without a stop, without a brown hand lifting

The tent-flap, or a bugle call at dawn,

Or ever on the long white road the flag

Of Jackson's quick brigades. I am alone,

Trapped, consenting, taken at last in mountains.

It is not the bugle now, or the long roll beating.[j]

The simple stroke of a chapel bell forbids

The hurtling dream, recalls the lonely wound.[k]

Young men, the God of your fathers is a just

[j] "From here on it is magnificent."
[k] "Does this mean Jackson? Or his own sorrow? If that why not *mind*?"

And merciful God who in this blood once shed	104
On your green altars measures out all days,	105
And measures out the grace	106
Whereby alone we live;	107
And in His might He waits,	108
Brooding within the certitude of time,	109
To bring this lost forsaken valor	110
And the fierce faith undying	111
And the love quenchless	112
To flower among the hills to which we cleave,	113
To fruit upon the mountains whither we flee,	114
Never forsaking, never denying	115
His children and His children's children forever	116
Unto all generations of the faithful heart. Amen.	117

Donald Davidson

Despite Tate's general approval of the poem, he wrote that he "must carp a little over details" because he thought in certain particulars the poem could be improved. In addition to the specific suggestions written on the manuscript itself, in his letter Tate commented in more detail on the opening passage.

> It seems to me that the opening lines are far too pat and abrupt. A more halting introduction to the theme, as if from the scattered im-

LEE IN THE MOUNTAINS
1865-1870

Walking into the shadows, walking alone
Where the sun falls through the ruined boughs of locusts,
Up to the president's office. Hearing the voices
Whisper, *Hush it is General Lee!*
But the soldiers' faces under the tossing flags
Lift no more by any road or field,
And I am spent with battle and old sorrow.
Walking the rocky path, where the steps decay
And the paint cracks and grass eats on the stone.
It is not General Lee, young men...
It is Robert Lee in a dark civilian suit who walks,
An outlaw fumbling for the latch, a voice
Commanding in a dream where no flag flies.

My father's house is taken and his hearth
Left to the candle-drippings where the ashes
Whirl at a chimney-breath on the cold stone.
I can hardly remember my father's look, I cannot
Answer his voice as he calls farewell in the misty
Mounting where riders gather at gates.
He was old then-- I was a child-- his hand
Held out for mine, some daybreak snatched away,
And he rode out, a beaten man. Now let
His lone grave keep, surer than cypress roots
The vow I made beside him. God too late
Unseals to certain eyes the drift
Of time and the hopes of men and a sacred cause.
The fortune of the Lees goes with this land

The first twenty-seven lines of Draft Four of "Lee in the Mountains," with Allen Tate's handwritten comments

ages of a moment a line of meditation suddenly took hold and went through to its end, is what you want. At present the opening is oratorical, almost set; but you want to make it dramatic.

Then in the forthright manner that was characteristic of the Fugitives' recommendations for improving a fellow poet's work, Tate proposes a major change in the opening of the poem. He points out, however, that he is not presenting a suggestion for Davidson to adopt literally. His rewriting of the opening lines merely attempts to demonstrate "what the dramatic effect might be":

> Walking in the shadows, walking alone . . .
> The sun falls through the ruined boughs of locusts
> Walk to the president's office . . .
>   The president!
> A boy mumbles *Hush it is General Lee!*
> The soldiers' faces under the tossing flags, etc., etc.,

As Tate had indicated earlier in the letter, his objections to the opening of the poem were that it was "too pat and abrupt." He is suggesting a "more halting introduction to the theme," and he proceeds to discuss his suggestion in more detail:

> And at the end of the passage why not interpolate a line or two or three of perfectly inconsequential observation on Lee's part. Make him see for a second a pile of rocks by the path, or a bush, on the fringe of his gathering meditation; even make the statement of this bold and flat. You have no idea what dramatic effect, what context it would give the whole poem. Powerful as the conclusion is, it would be twice again as powerful. You have let Lee speak but you have not let us see him. Just make him say: I must have those rocks moved; or that spirea will bloom in two weeks, it should have been trimmed; or anything like that.

That Tate had shown the poem to Caroline Gordon and discussed the proposed change with her is revealed by the paragraph he added as a postscript to the letter.

> Caroline thinks the dramatic effect might be achieved by having him address the casual remarks to some boys standing by. . . . I might add that while such an interpolation would be outside your "form," it would really by its slight violence establish the form. The interpolated passage might even be put into parenthesis.

The Evolution of "Lee in the Mountains"

Davidson's reaction to Tate's suggestions is revealed most dramatically in the revisions which he made after he received Tate's letter and marginal comments. Obviously following Tate's suggestion, Davidson attempted to provide a "more halting introduction to the theme" by giving a paragraph break at the end of line three and by adding a three-line passage that begins in the middle of line five:

> Good morning, boys.
> (Don't get up. You are early. It is long
> Before the bell. You will have long to wait
> On these cold steps. . . .)

Tate had pointed out that the opening of the poem should be more dramatic and that Davidson could make it more dramatic by letting Lee speak without violating the unity of form (the poem is an interior monologue). Tate gives Caroline Gordon's suggestion that the remarks be addressed to some boys standing by and adds that "the interpolated passage might even be put into parenthesis." Up to this point, it is clear that the poet followed these suggestions to the letter.

One can see, however, that Davidson did not accept completely Tate's recommendations, though it is obvious that Tate's comments stimulated the creative activity that greatly strengthened the first section of the poem. Tate suggested that Lee's remarks be "casual" and "inconsequential," that his observations—though "directed to the students"—be unrelated to the primary matters of the poem. But Lee's remarks, as Davidson presents them, are undeniably related to the rest of the poem; in fact, at the outset they suggest clearly and forcefully its essential conflict. As Lee walks toward his office he is observed by the students who are awaiting the bell that will summon them to the morning assembly. When he approaches the steps where they sit, one student respectfully hushes the noise of their conversation and all of them rise and speak to General Lee. The man formerly a general and now a college president speaks, tells his students not to rise, and makes the casual and polite comments that one would expect from him: "You are early. It is long / Before the bell. You will have long to wait / On these cold steps. . . ." The reason for Lee's speaking has been explained and the persons to whom he speaks have been identified; consequently, the reader is not surprised that his visit inside Lee's mind has been interrupted.

Furthermore, the reader is soon aware that Lee's apparently casual remarks are significant. Not only will the students have long to wait before the bell announces the opening of the daily devotions, but also they must await the coming of a new era to the South. Although Lee realizes, as Davidson indicates in the next line of the poem, that "the young have time to wait," it is clear that Lee, "spent with old wars and new sorrow," has not. What he can do, he must do now. In this interpolated passage, then, the poet is able to present Lee's predicament with force and clarity. The reader shares the dilemma Lee faces in his struggles with the problem that confronts him: Stripped of all authority, an outlaw in his own land, how can he continue to act honorably and at the same time strengthen in the young the courage to persevere—to maintain their integrity and self-respect and their belief in the enduring virtues of the society that produced them, and to retain their courage when all they value seems "maimed, defeated, lost, impugned"? This conflict, dramatically suggested in Lee's brief comments to the students seated on the cold steps, is resolved in the concluding section of the poem.

Davidson also considers seriously Tate's other suggestions. In line 7, Tate had underlined "old" and asked in the margin "More definite?" The poet changes the line that appeared in Draft Four as "And I am spent with battle and old sorrow" to "And I am spent with old wars and new sorrow." In line 32 ("Her voice comes back a filmy distillation"), "filmy" was encircled with the comment "omit adjective?"; Davidson substitutes for it "murmuring." "Splendors" was underlined in line 33 ("Of old Virginia splendors done to death") and "Is this word in character?" was asked. Davidson alters the line to "Of old Virginia times now faint and gone." In line 44 ("And never heard the long Confederate war-cry") Tate had suggested the deletion of "war," and the suggestion is followed. Tate's comments on lines 75 and 76 indicated genuine concern: "*Sword* too conventional. Not dramatic, but oratorical and I think out of Lee's psychology. Preceding lines so good they deserve better than this." In Draft Four these lines are:

> The sword
> Locks in its sheath, the sword of Robert Lee
> Bows to the rust that cankers and the silence.

Davidson changes them to:

> The pen
> Turns to the waiting page, the sword
> Bows to the rust that cankers and the silence.

Tate also objected to "wound" in line 101 ("the hurtling dream, recalls the lonely wound"), and, as Tate had suggested, Davidson substitutes "mind."

In attempting to emphasize that his appreciation of his friend's poetic achievement is objective, Tate wrote:

> At first I thought (not wishing to give you the benefit of any doubt whatever) that I might be moved too much by the subject as such. But that was not the case. It will be the chief ornament of our A.R. exhibit.

Tate's reference is to the *American Review* for which he was at that time preparing a poetry supplement. "Lee in the Mountains" was included in that supplement—along with poems by Randall Jarrell, Howard Baker, Robert Penn Warren, John Gould Fletcher, Janet Lewis, John Peale Bishop, Mark Van Doren, Louis Macneice, Manson Radford, and John Crowe Ransom—and was first published in the *American Review* for May, 1934. There are five variants between that version and the one included in *Lee in the Mountains and Other Poems* (Boston, 1938). Although none of the changes is major, they do indicate the poet's continuing concern, even after the poem had appeared in print, that his conceptions not "outrun [his] execution in this poem."

(*American Review*)	The tossing flags	9
(Houghton Mifflin)	Their tossing flags	
(AR)	Where the steps decay	12
(HM)	Where steps decay	
(AR)	Lapped in a haze of light.	62
(HM)	Crowned with a haze of light	
(AR)	Obedient to a soldier's trust—to sink, to lie	67

(HM)　　Obedient to a soldier's trust? to lie
(AR)　　Unto all generations of the faithful　121
　　　　heart. Amen.
(HM)　　Unto all generations of the faithful
　　　　heart.

Everyone is well aware of the dangers involved in trying to describe the creative process. There are, perhaps, as many different procedures as there are poets, or maybe the process varies with each poem, each work of art dictating its own mode of creation. Generally speaking, however, in the creation of "Lee in the Mountains," Davidson seems to have followed an orderly and logical procedure, one that can be detected in the four extant drafts of the poem written before it appeared in print.[14] In creating his best-known poem, Davidson apparently proceeded in a manner somewhat as follows. For many years a supporter of the principles exemplified by Lee as citizen, soldier, and leader, Davidson was thoroughly acquainted with the facts—and with the many interpretations of these facts—that relate to Lee's illustrious career. It appears evident, furthermore, that he had a firm conception of the materials he would use in the entire poem before he began the actual process of composition, because the contents of the sixty-one lines of Draft One remain essentially unchanged in all the subsequent revisions. However, when he was forced to put the poem aside for a few weeks in order to return to Vanderbilt for the opening of the fall quarter, he carefully reworked the language of the completed segment—line by line—before attempting to finish the poem. Then he added the sixty-nine lines that completed Draft Two and, in this draft, included essentially all the subject matter that appears in the published version of the poem. Draft Three constitutes the most thorough of the revisions of form and style. Although new brief passages are added and a few existing ones are dropped, the poet's primary concern is obviously with matters of expression—searching for the exact word or phrase, sharpening the imagery, or increasing textural richness. Although Draft Four contains

---

14. These four drafts can be found in the Jesse E. Wills Fugitive/Agrarian Collection, Special Collections, Jean and Alexander Heard Library, Vanderbilt University.

some interesting and significant emendations, they are not as significant as those in the earlier revisions because they were made, for the most part, during the actual process of typewriting a manuscript for Allen Tate's perusal and for presentation to the meeting of the United Daughters of the Confederacy.

The number and kind of the revisions made after Davidson received Tate's letter and comments reveal the seriousness with which the poet regarded the suggestions of his friend and critic. An examination of the extant drafts of "Lee in the Mountains" and of the Tate comments demonstrates concretely the manner in which the criticism of the Fugitive Group assisted its member poets in their creative efforts; this examination may also give some insight into the mysterious process of creativity itself.

(1965)

Brother to Dragons:
A Meditation on the Basic Nature of Man

AT "Rocky Hill," the home of Lilburne Lewis, the son of Lucy Jefferson Lewis and her husband, Colonel Charles Lewis, on the night of December 15, 1811, Lilburne and his younger brother, Isham, mutilated, killed, and burned the body of a young slave, John, for a very frivolous reason. Robert Penn Warren was surprised to find that there was no reference to this atrocious act in any of the published or unpublished writings of Thomas Jefferson. In fact, as far as Warren could determine, Jefferson had never referred, even in conversation, to the evil deeds of his sister's two sons. What really concerned Warren, he wrote at the time of this discovery, was that apparently Jefferson, "the prophet of human perfectibility," could not bring himself to confront "this evidence of human depravity" in the hearts of members of his own family.[1]

This fact kept tantalizing his imagination, Warren reports, so he began to think of it as material for a novel. On his next visit to Kentucky, in the summer of 1946, he and his father went in search of what was left of the Lewis home. Just outside of Smithfield, a small village about fifteen miles east of Paducah, he found a sign, erected by the DAR in 1924, directing him to the home of the sister of the third president of the United States. He drove north one and a half miles to the mountain "which can be seen in the distance," as the sign directs, found the mountain and climbed it in the July heat (pp. 16–25). When he finally arrived at what was left of the house site, he found:

This essay originally appeared, in slightly different form, in *Mississippi Quarterly*, XXXVII (Spring, 1984). Reprinted by permission of the editor.

1. Robert Penn Warren, *Brother to Dragons: A Tale in Verse and Voices* (New York, 1979), x–xiii. Hereinafter cited by page number in the text.

> There was the quiet, high glade,
> Blue grass set round with beeches, quietest tree.
> The air was suddenly sweet, a hint of cool,
> I stood in the new silence and heard my heart.
> And there it was: the huddled stones of ruin,
> Just the foundation and the tumbled chimneys,
> To say the human hand, once here, had gone,
> And never would come back.
>
> (p. 23)

When he returned to his study and began to work with the historical material, he found that it did not have the "structure of a novel," it did not "fulfill itself circumstantially"; neither, he felt, could a novel "bear the burden of the authorial commentary necessary to interpret the material." Then he tried to use the historical information, which he had come to view "almost obsessively," in a drama. Again he found the facts could not be interpreted intelligibly in that genre. As he tried to convert the material into a drama, with Jefferson and a chorus as commentators, a plot problem developed: The role of Jefferson, he soon realized, would assume a commanding and disproportionate importance. Then he turned to poetry, first trying the folk ballad. Again, he felt, the form did not allow for sufficient interpretation of the material.[2] Then he turned to a dramatic monologue, set at an unspecified time and place (at "no time," in "any place"). Trying to keep a dramatic relation between the eighteenth and twentieth centuries, he added R. P. W., a typical, inquisitive, modern man. Jefferson, Warren says, is the protagonist as the reader views him in the mortal throes of trying to "come to terms with the appearance of depravity in his own family." The artistic problem of finding appropriate "symbols and language" to ex-

---

2. He has even preserved part of the ballad:
> *The two brothers sat by the sagging fire,*
> *Lilburne and Isham sat by the fire,*
> *For it was lonesome weather*
> *"Isham," said Lilburne, "shove the jug nigher,*
> *For it is lonesome weather.*
> *For it is lonesome weather in Kentucky,*
> *For Mammy's dead and the log burns low*
> *And the wind is raw and it's coming snow*
> *And the woods lean close and Virginia's far*
> *And the night is dark and never a star . . ."*
>
> (p. 31)

press "suitably the views of the different characters" and at the same time "to keep interest and readability at the level of action and debate" was so profound that it took Warren six years to finish the version of the poem he published in 1953. Still not satisfied with the manner in which he had expressed and interpreted the characters' reactions to the central issue, he kept the poem on his work table and kept revising it.[3] In 1979 he published "another and very different version," which he calls a "new work": "Now there are a number of cuts made from the original version and some additions. Meriwether [Lewis] is given a more significant role. There is, in large measure, a significant change of rhythm. A number of dramatic effects are sharpened. Though the basic action and theme remain the same, there is, I trust, an important difference in the total 'feel'" (p. xiv).[4]

The poem, as James H. Justus has pointed out, is a significant work in Warren's artistic career:

> An accurate description of *Brother to Dragons* is that which the poet himself used to describe "Billie Potts"—a "bridge piece," a

---

3. Robert Penn Warren, "The Way *Brother to Dragons* Was Written," in Neil Nakadate (ed.), *Robert Penn Warren: Critical Perspectives* (Lexington, Ky., 1981), 212–13; Victor Strandberg, "*Brother to Dragons* and the Craft of Revision," in James A. Grimshaw, Jr. (ed.), *Robert Penn Warren's "Brother to Dragons": A Discussion* (Baton Rouge, 1983), 200–210.

4. Margaret Mills Harper, "Versions of History and *Brother to Dragons*," in Grimshaw (226–43), lists and discusses the difference between the 1953 and the 1979 versions:

1. The 1953 version is 4,387 lines; the 1979 is 3,699.
2. The "relived blank verse of the 1953 version has been broken and syncopated through deletions and divisions."
3. The rhetorical advantages that R. P. W. had over Jefferson in the 1953 version have been decreased. No longer can R. P. W. interrupt or correct the great man, and his "smugness" is much less evident.
4. As Warren mentions in his introduction to the 1979 version, Meriwether Lewis' role has been much expanded.
5. Although Warren insists in an interview with Professor Floyd C. Watkins that he had not read Boynton Merrill's *Jefferson's Nephews* (Princeton, 1976) until after he had completed the new version of the poem, many of the inaccuracies and half-truths of the 1953 version have been corrected: (a) Charles Lewis is not referred to as a physician; (b) the spelling of Lilburne's and Letitia's names have been corrected; (c) Meriwether is referred to only as a cousin of the two Lewis brothers (not first cousin); (d) Lilburne is not identified as the firstborn son of Charles and Lucy Jefferson Lewis; (e) John's monetary value is increased from three hundred dollars to the more realistic five hundred dollars; (f) Lilburne is not murdered; his death is accidental suicide.

"jumping-off place"—when he began writing poems after a ten-year silence. . . . The term *bridge piece* suggests not only access from one point to another but also a solidification and accrual of attitudes, images, modes, and aesthetic devices. . . . If it points the way that the future work would take, *Brother to Dragons* is also a formal and thematic culmination. Recurrent figures show up in sometimes exacerbated ways: the man faced with his own inexplicable nature; the betrayer and the betrayed fulfilling the mysterious compulsions for completeness in each other; the cynical observer-narrator whose own urgencies for order and meaning erupt within and parallel to those of others.[5]

In many of Warren's novels published before *Brother to Dragons* he had employed interpolated narratives to point up the plight of the protagonists—their confusion, purposelessness, the lack of aim and direction in their lives. In the first novel, *Night Rider* (1939), only Willie Proudfit, the hero of the interpolated narrative, is able to find some purpose in his life. In *At Heaven's Gate* (1943), Ashby Wyndham, though not as convincingly portrayed as Willie, is the only character to gain self-knowledge so that he is able to function as a human being in a modern technocratic society. Cass Mastern, whose story on the surface seems to have so little to do with the situation in which Jack Burden finds himself that it was deleted from one British edition of *All the King's Men*, serves as a plausible model for his modern kinsman and enables him to unify the fragmentary chaos of his life. In his poetry, too, Warren uses a similar technique to demonstrate the inevitable clash of incongruous elements, the most notable example being "The Ballad of Billie Potts" (1943). In this poem Warren uses a simple folktale to point up the error in American thought of the nineteenth century—that renewal and a new innocence, a chance to begin again, lay in "The Journey West."[6] The American thought for years was that one could ride away "from *goodbye, goodbye* and toward *hello*," that "like the cicada" he could leave the "old shell of self" behind.[7] Although this was the philosophic attitude that Warren wished to explode, he realized that the spare, uncompli-

---

5. James H. Justus, *The Achievement of Robert Penn Warren* (Baton Rouge, 1981), 63.
6. For a complete discussion of the concept, see Joe Davis, "Robert Penn Warren and The Journey to the West," *Modern Fiction Studies*, VI (1960), 73–82.
7. Robert Penn Warren, *Selected Poems, 1923–1975* (New York, 1977), 274.

cated form of the folk ballad, developed to move a narrative briskly along, was not appropriate to allow him to interpret the significance of the Billie Potts story. As in the novels, therefore, he interpolated within this narrative authorial, parenthetical commentary in the richly textural style of the early poems:

> (There is always another country and always another place.
> There is always another name and another face.
> And the name and the face are you, and you
> The name and the face, and the stream you gaze into
> Will show the adoring face, show the lips that lift to you
> As you lean with the implacable thirst of self,
> As you lean to the image which is yourself, . . .
> To drink not of the stream but of your deep identity,
> But water is water and it flows,
> Under the image on the water the water coils and goes
> And its own beginning and its end only the water knows. . . .)
>
> (pp. 276–77)

As Warren carries into *Brother* some of the techniques used in the earlier poetry, he also reiterates some of the themes and motifs of the earlier work. In *Eleven Poems on the Same Theme* (1942), Warren had explored the possibility of delineating the division of the modern sensibility in psychological terms. In one of his earliest poems, "Return: An Elegy," as Victor Strandberg points out, there is the suggestion of man's being confronted with omnipresent evil, "some dark guilt that is rising to stain the soul beyond any power of will to stop it."[8] Strandberg reminds us that Jung has commented on the significance of the separation of the conscious rational mind, the source of the knowledge of naturalistic reality, from the unconscious, irrational mind, the means of acquiring intuitive, instinctive knowledge. "Separation from his instinctual nature," Jung warns, "inevitably plunges civilized man into the conflict between conscious and unconscious, spirit and nature, knowledge and faith, a split that becomes pathological the moment his consciousness is no longer able to neglect or suppress his instinctual side."[9] In "Crime," the demoniac killer, the instinctive self, cannot remember the crime he

---

8. Victor H. Strandberg, *The Poetic Vision of Robert Penn Warren* (Lexington, Ky., 1977), 131.
9. Quoted *ibid.*, 137.

has committed. He knows neither the victim nor the motive. Despite the vileness of his crime, he maintains an innocence that "you," the conscious self, can never regain. The real crime in the poem is the conscious self's attempt to destroy what Jung called "humanity's black collective shadow." "What the mad killer did in frenzy," Strandberg argues, "*you* did in vanity," a dramatic statement of the difference between Jefferson's crime and Lilburne Lewis'.[10]

In "Original Sin: A Short Story," the secret instinctive self is persistent in its attempts to make "you," the rational conscious self, aware of its existence.

> Nodding, its great head rattling like a gourd,
> And locks like seaweed strung on the stinking stone,
> The nightmare stumbles past, and you have heard
> It fumble your door before it whimpers and is gone:
> It acts like the old hound that used to snuffle your door and moan.[11]

You thought it was connected with a wen on your grandfather's forehead, so you thought "you had lost it when you left Omaha," but "you met it in Harvard Yard as the historic steeple / Was confirming the midnight with its hideous racket." So you discover that nothing is lost; it can neither "be escaped from, repudiated," nor "exorcised."[12] *You* may try to forget "original sin" but only when *you* acknowledge its existence can *you* discover *your* true identity.

The source of Warren's title, *Brother to Dragons*, is Job 30:29: "I am brother to dragons and a companion to owls." Job is a God-fearing man: He has lived an upright life, paid allegiance to his God, and tried to follow his commandments. He cannot understand, therefore, why he has to suffer. His is a sin of pride or, to express his dilemma in psychological terms, he has forgotten his instinctive, unconscious self, the collective unconscious, or, to return to the theological, the universal guilt of "original sin," in which he shares with all other men. His redemption does not come until he admits that he is "brother to dragons and a companion to owls." Jefferson's sin is that of Job. A true child of the Enlightenment, he believed in the perfectibility of man.

10. *Ibid.*, 142.
11. Warren, *Selected Poems, 1923–1975*, 288.
12. Strandberg, *Poetic Vision of Robert Penn Warren*, 143.

At Philadelphia during the Constitutional Convention he saw among the delegates "individual evil," but his reason told him "it is only provisional paradox," and it will "resolve itself in Time" (p. 7). Right reason and common sense persuaded him that man is a rational creature with the inclination to do right. Any other course of action is irrational. When man discovers his aberrations, his mistakes, he will correct them, and sometime in the future, perfect men will live in a perfect society. It was this belief that prompted him to send his "near son," Meriwether Lewis, into the wilderness as a torchbearer, bringing civilization to the barbarians to assist in ushering in the millennium. It was this conviction that made Jefferson unable to accept Lilburne Lewis' unprovoked act of depravity. Jefferson's belief in abstract good, as Meriwether expresses it, made him responsible for the great lie: the insistence that man is capable both of the great brotherhood and of justice. His naïveté made Jefferson unaware of the forces of evil that always lie just beneath the level of the unconscious. Regardless of how carefully man is trained or how rigidly he attempts to control himself, he is always capable of an irrational act of evil.

Like Willie Stark in *All the King's Men,* Jefferson is a man of action; he can "err massively," but unlike Stark, he has the sensitivity to recognize his transgressions.[13] One major development of the narrative is Jefferson's struggle to understand the nature of his errors and his attempts to overcome them. Another aspect of the plot is the development of the interpolated narrator, R. P. W. A cynical, pragmatic modern man at the beginning of the poem, he simply believes that Jefferson refuses to confront the existence of undeniable and persistent evil, despite the evidences of it in his own family, in order to maintain his concept of abstract goodness. Just as Jefferson changes from naïve optimism to pessimism to transcendent irony, R. P. W. moves from cynicism to indifference to affirmation.[14] At the beginning of the poem, Jefferson, the man of idea, like Adam Stanton of *All the King's Men,* is inclined to see man either as an angel or a beast, whereas R. P. W., cynical, nihilistic, and agnostic, is unable to

---

13. Justus, *Achievement of Robert Penn Warren,* 64.
14. For evidence of R. P. W.'s development, see Dennis Dooley, "The Persona R. P. W. in Warren's *Brother to Dragons,*" *Mississippi Quarterly,* XXV (1971), 19–30.

A Meditation on the Basic Nature of Man

find much hope for the future of man. As his experiences in the poem affect him, however, as Mark Royden Winchell points out, he comes to function as a ballast to the negativisms of our age by becoming, in R. W. B. Lewis' term, "A Party of Irony."[15]

In the beginning of the poem, Jefferson's view of humanity is so badly shaken—he finds Lilburne's act so repulsive—that he regards man as a beast:

> And thus my minotaur. There at the blind
> Labyrinthine turn of my personal time—
> .... —yes, then met
> The beast, in beauty masked. And the time
> I met it was—at least, it seems so now—
> That moment when the first alacrity
> Of blood stumbles, and all natural joy
> Sees Nature but as a mirror for its natural doom.
> (pp. 7–8)

At the time he was helping to found the nation, his view of man as a whole was angelic, though he was able to see in individual men slight inconsequential imperfections:

> Philadelphia, yes. I knew we were only men,
> Defined in our errors and interests. But I, a man too—
> Yes, laugh if you will—stumbled into
> The breathless awe of vision, saw sudden
> On every face, face after face,
> Bleared, puffed, lank, lean red-fleshed or sallow, all—
> On all saw the brightness blaze, . . .
> And my heart cried out:
> "Oh, this is Man!"
> (p. 7)

In this innocent naïve period, Jefferson, as Winchell has reminded us, employs architectural analogies to reveal his view of man. He finds the Gothic sculpture of Paris abhorrent:

> from every
> Porch, pillar, and portal stared
> Beaked visage of unworkable evil, and
> Fat serpents fanged themselves

---

15. Mark Royden Winchell, "Robert Penn Warren's *Brother to Dragons:* Irony and Image of Man," *Mississippi Quarterly,* XXXV (1981–82), 15–25.

> To the genitals of women, whose stone eyes bulged out
> As to distribute sightlessness on all, and the hacked mouth
> Gave no scream you could hear from across long time, and
> Vile parodies and mock-shows of the human shape
> That might be beasts but yet were men.
>
> (p. 27)

He much preferred the classical order and grace of the Maison Quarrée at Nîmes:

> I saw the law of Rome and the light
> Of just proportion and heart's harmony.
> And I said: "Here is a shape that shines, set
> On a grundel of Nature's law, a rooftree
> So innocent of imprecision
> That a man may enter in to find his freedom
> Like air breathed, and all his mind
> Would glow like a coal under bellows.
>
> (p. 92)

Not only is Warren's view of the beast image, despite his cynicism, more accurate than Jefferson's because he does not share Jefferson's feeling of outrage and revulsion, but he develops the Job analogy suggested by the title. On his first visit to the Lewis ruins, he is very much aware of the wasteland that his fellow Americans have made of the land of opportunity. He is pleased that he does not have to remain there to view the desolation. Like all other moderns he is mobile; all he has to do is "touch the accelerator and quick you're gone / Beyond forgiveness, pity, hope, hate, love" (p. 12). His attitude toward the desolation he sees around him is best revealed when he answers Eliot's call for "water, water," to revive the wasteland, by stopping "to void the bladder," and then rushing on while the silence is broken by the screaming of the July flies "like a nerve gone wild / And then a million / Took up the job, and in the simultaneous outrage / Sunlight screamed, while urine pattered the parched soil" (pp. 12–13).

Finally he arrives at the ruins of the Lewis home, climbs the mountain, walks down the road that had been made by "Black Hands" and "black sweat," views from afar "the huddled stones of ruin, / Just the foundation and the tumbled chimneys." Then he walks closer to what remains of the house, "and then / It happened":

> You know,
> When you have clambered hard and fought the brush
> And breath comes short and both lungs full of cotton,
> And shirt is soaked and holds your hide like glue,
> And heat runs prickling in your blood like ants—
> Then if you stop, even in sun-blaze,
> It's like malaria shook your bones like dice.
>
> Well, standing there, I'd felt, I guess, the first
> Faint tremor of that natural chill, but then,
> In some deep aperture among the stones,
> I saw the eyes, their glitter in that dark,
> And suddenly the heat thrust forth, and the fat, black
> Body, molten, out-flowed, as though those stones
> Bled forth earth's inner darkness to the day.
>
> (pp. 23–24)

The serpent, Warren notes, is taller than he; he is transfixed by "the soiled white of belly bulge," the "black side scales," and "the swollen head hung / Haloed and high in light." He instinctively associates the serpent with the archetypical myths of the Garden of Eden, with Apophis, in Egyptian mythology the power of darkness against whom the sun god waged war daily, and with Nidhogg, "whose cumbrous coils and cold dung chill / The root of the world's tree." Almost before he thinks consciously of these theological or psychological interpretations, including the possibility that this serpent might be a "symbol of that black lust all men fear and long for," he sees that it is merely a common variety of snake—called variously "Black Snake, Black Pilot Snake, the Mountain Blacksnake / Hog-snout or Chicken Snake"—with the scientific name *"Elaphe obsoleta obsoleta."* He remembers that it is "not to be confused with the Black Racer, / *Coluber constrictor*"; then his reason reminds him that the black snake's primary naturalistic function is to kill rats (pp. 24–25). Although he concludes that it is "just a snake," its reappearance in the poem convinces the reader it is more than that.

The third person to whom the monster appears is Lilburne, who, many commentators agree, is not subhuman, as Jefferson believes, but a badly disturbed human being motivated by a dominating Oedipal complex and a compelling sadistic impulse. It is also likely, as Strandberg argues, that Lilburne "does embody personally that dimension of unconscious evil which the serpent symbolizes and which is present in every man."[16] But Jefferson persists almost to the very end in refusing to admit his kinship to the evil Lilburne; he will not take Lilburne's hand with the blood still "slick" on it (p. 116). Jefferson's reason, which is not the faculty through which one can conquer irrational fear, is combatted by Lucy's light, love, the understanding of the human heart. In Allen Tate's phrase, she has "knowledge carried to the heart." Finally, like Job, Jefferson learns humility: He knows he is "brother to dragons," that one cannot live by reason alone; he demonstrates his awareness that he has within him the same impulses that caused Lilburne to commit his evil deed. He touches Lilburne and proclaims that knowledge is "the bitter bread. / I have eaten the bitter bread. / In joy, would end" (p. 120).

If Jefferson learns humility from Job, it is "Lucretius' admonition," as Justus says, "that the terrors of darkness must be banished not by sunlight but by 'the aspect and law of nature' [that] lies behind R. P. W.'s rehabilitation."[17] As the highest creature in the natural order, man must assume a proper attitude toward nature; he must always regard it as a contingent and mysterious force, one that he should never presume to look upon as merely existing to perform solely for man's benefit.

The thematic concerns of *Brother to Dragons* are not essentially different from those of some of Warren's other work—especially *Eleven Poems on the Same Theme*, "The Ballad of Billie Potts," and *All the King's Men*—but as Warren has said, completing this poem reinvigorated him with "a whole new sense of poetry.... The narrative sense began to enter the lyric poems."[18] This kind of cross-breeding was the "germ" that produced *Promises*. Perhaps the most meaningful statement one can make about *Brother to Dragons* is that Lucy Jefferson Lewis is as instrumental in R. P. W.'s transformation as she is in Jefferson's. Her "light" gives Warren hope, as his awareness in the collective unconscious gives him a belief in transcendence. Aesthetically, *Brother to Dragons* is one of Warren's most satisfying creations.

(1984)

16. Strandberg, *Poetic Vision of Robert Penn Warren*, 174.
17. Justus, *Achievement of Robert Penn Warren*, 66–67.
18. Floyd C. Watkins and John T. Hiers (eds.), *Robert Penn Warren Talking: Interviews, 1950–1978* (New York, 1980), 189.

"The Lady Ageth but Is Not Stoop'd": Agrarianism in Contemporary Southern Fiction

DONALD DAVIDSON once observed that *I'll Take My Stand* (1930), the manifesto of the Nashville Agrarians, was perhaps the "most misunderstood book in American literature, read or unread." Contrary to a widely held conviction, the twelve men who contributed to that symposium did not propose a kind of utopian conservatism; they did not believe—though they clearly wished—that they could destroy the realities of a mechanistic materialism. Instead, they set out to defend the life and values of a traditional society from the forces of uncurbed acquisitive materialism that were bent on transforming the established social order at whatever cost. They were attempting, as Richard Weaver has pointed out, to present an "effective challenge to a monolithic culture of unredeemed materialism." They did not wish to turn the clock back. They were not visionaries unable to live in the present, and they well knew that the kind of agrarian society that had once been the foundation of American democracy could never be again. However, they did employ every rhetorical means at their disposal, and there were many, to emphasize the dangers confronting a society that had unwittingly decided "to invest . . . [its] economic resources in the applied sciences."[1]

"'The Lady Ageth but Is Not Stoop'd': Agrarianism in Contemporary Southern Fiction," by T. D. Young, from *Literature and the Visual Arts in Contemporary Society* (Columbus: Ohio State University Press, 1985), is reprinted by permission. © 1985 by the Ohio State University Press. All rights reserved.

1. Twelve Southerners, *I'll Take My Stand: The South and the Agrarian Tradition* (New York, 1930); Richard M. Weaver, *The Southern Tradition at Bay: A History of Postbellum Thought* (New York, 1968), 391.

In fact, as Louis D. Rubin, Jr., has argued, *I'll Take My Stand* "makes no real economic proposals for dispensing with the machine age; it hardly even defines what agrarianism is, other than something involving a society in which farming is of importance; it says a great deal about what is wrong with industrialism, but almost nothing about how to get rid of it."[2] The Nashville Agrarians, it is true, were outraged by human attempts to deify the machine, by the conviction that a technocratic society was inevitable, and by the creation of an intellectual climate that denies individual freedom of choice, a climate in which humanistic values cannot exist.

It is now generally understood, I believe, that despite the broad area of general agreement, many of the contributors to this basic document of modern agrarian thought had different expectations of what they hoped would accrue from their involvement in the movement. Donald Davidson was deeply concerned that modern society, in his opinion, was being forced to accept in the name of progress values that were inferior to those it was giving up. John Crowe Ransom attempted to point out the superiority of what he called a "mature society," one that nurtures *both* the "economic values" (the means of earning a living) and the "aesthetic values" (the means of civilized living). No society, Ransom insisted, "has ever lived without a poetry, and we should not expect ours to be an exception." He wanted, in short, a social order in which the arts were a means of communication, not just superfluous decoration. Allen Tate has written that the purpose of his essay in the symposium was to attempt to convince his readers of the urgent need for a return to religious humanism. Andrew Lytle's admittedly idealistic essay argued that every individual must do everything possible in the attempt to retain personal freedom. At the Fugitive reunion in Nashville in 1956, Robert Penn Warren indicated he was attracted to the movement because of his concern about the "disintegration of the notion of the individual in the society we're living in."

All were apparently in agreement, in the words of William Pratt, that "a fully satisfying way of life cannot be produced by economic forces, with their shifting cycles of poverty and

---

2. Louis D. Rubin, Jr. *The Wary Fugitive: Four Poets and the South* (Baton Rouge, 1978), 235.

wealth. . . . [Such a way of life] can only come from an adherence to stable human values and ideals. . . . The unchecked exploitation of nature can become suicidally destructive, when the very air we breathe and the water we drink have become poisoned by rampant urbanism and industrialism." Professor Pratt concludes that the Nashville Agrarians were censoring the abuses of an age.[3]

Despite significant differences—the Agrarians would be skeptical of inner voices proclaiming their divinity and the suggestion that each person should march to the beat of a different drummer—the Nashville Agrarians were arguing for some of the same values that unified the New England transcendentalists. A hundred and fifty years ago, Emerson was deploring the fact that "things are in the saddle and ride mankind." His disciple, Henry David Thoreau, was convinced that "the mass of men lead lives of quiet desperation." He went to Walden Pond to prove "a man is rich in proportion to the number of things he can afford to do without," and the "cost of a thing is the amount of what I call life which is required to be exchanged for it."[4] As Thoreau and Emerson did more than a hundred years ago, the Agrarians warned that American social forms were emphasizing too many of the wrong values. Ransom insists, for example, that any society that invests the bulk of its resources in the applied sciences in an attempt "to improve the world" is one that thrusts its citizens on a treadmill, in search of a perfection that has always eluded them and always will.

If the preceding brief summary may be taken as a satisfactory statement of some of the basic aims of the Nashville Agrarians—and if the Nashville Agrarians are accepted as an adequate representation of modern agrarianism—it is easy to detect evidences of agrarian thought in contemporary Southern fiction. Conspicuously absent in the fiction are echoes of the North Carolina Planners, a liberal group contemporary with the Nashville conservatives, one headed by Howard Odum and his colleagues at

---

3. Quoted in M. Thomas Inge, "The Continuing Relevance of *I'll Take My Stand*," *Mississippi Quarterly*, XXXIII (Fall, 1980), 456–57.

4. Henry David Thoreau, *Walden* and "Civil Disobedience" (New York, 1966), 61.

the Institute for Research in Social Science, who argued that the South would not be, in Franklin D. Roosevelt's language, "the Nation's No. 1 economic problem" if the section would adopt a carefully planned economy that would effect "a working balance between nature's endowment and its use."[5] The Agrarians believed that such an economy could never be developed because to do so would require that people harness the power of nature and turn it to their uses and benefits. Such a view of nature, however, Ransom warned in the Introduction to *I'll Take My Stand*, is highly simplified. When people have an illusion of "having power over nature," they lose the sense of nature as something "mysterious and contingent." Neither is there in contemporary Southern fiction any great attraction for an omnipotent and compassionate Uncle Sam, for whom the Joad family yearned with such great fervor in *The Grapes of Wrath* (1939).

What greatly concerned the Agrarians was modern man's willingness to accept a poor imitation for genuine human living. They also seriously doubted the social planners' ability to effect a perfect society, as in the vision of an all-powerful federal government's detecting and meeting the needs of all people everywhere. As they looked around them, they could see many involved programs of social and economic improvement—some of which were well-intentioned schemes to raise the standard of living—going awry and resulting, too often, in a decline in the quality of life. These concerns, which dominated Agrarian thought in 1930, can be found in a large quantity of modern fiction.

In 1930, Andrew Lytle warned that farmers who falter in their efforts to remain self-sufficient and enter the race for wealth by growing one money crop are racing toward destruction. They must deny the enticements of industry or they will lose not only their farms but their identity and independence as well.[6] As the farm becomes mechanized, there is no work for the sons and daughters there, so they move to the neighboring village, where they become waitresses and service station employees. After a

---

5. Howard W. Odum, *Southern Regions of the United States* (Chapel Hill, 1936), 23–25.

6. Andrew Lytle, "The Hind Tit," in Twelve Southerners, *I'll Take My Stand*, 234–35.

farm family has acquired a tractor, they buy a truck and a car. They install a Delco plant for heating and lighting. Finally, they neglect their gardens and raise fewer of the cattle they need to slaughter for home consumption. The family has become completely consumed in a finance economy, and they are soon defeated because they cannot control the elements that grow the crops; therefore they cannot pay the bank the money they owe. They cannot make the sun shine or the rain fall to make the crop mature or prevent the cold wind or falling hail from destroying it. Despite the use of insecticides that poison the food as well as the pests, the insects are still with them. Because they cannot control these variables, their crop is not predictable; their income, therefore, is uncertain, but their debts are not. Finally the bank will foreclose on the farm in order to get the money it must have to stay in business. The farmer has no alternative; he must join his sons and daughters in the village—if physically able, at the service station; if not, on relief.

Farmers must deny themselves, says Lytle, the material objects that industry must sell them:

> Throw out the radio and take down the fiddle from the wall. Forsake the movies for the play parties and square dances. And turn away from the liberal capons who fill the pulpits as preachers. Seek a priesthood that may manifest the will and intelligence to renounce science and search out the Word in the authorities. . . .
>
> So long as . . . [man] lives in a divided world he is rendered impotent in the defense of his natural economy and inherited life. He has been turned into the runt pig in a sow's litter. Squeezed and tricked out of the best place at the side, he is forced to take the hind tit for nourishment.[7]

The children and grandchildren of Lytle's displaced farmers have been a matter of Peter Taylor's primary concern for more than forty years. The protagonist of a Peter Taylor story is often a resident of a middle-sized city of the upper South, though almost always one or two generations removed from a small Southern town, usually the fictional Thornton, Tennessee.[8] Born into a successful, well-to-do family that has furnished Tennessee with two governors, Peter Taylor comes by his agrarian sentiments

---

7. *Ibid.*, 244–45.
8. Peter Taylor, *The Collected Stories* (New York, 1969), 252.

honestly. He attended Southwestern-at-Memphis, Vanderbilt, and Kenyon, where he followed John Crowe Ransom in 1937. Later he enrolled in graduate school at Louisiana State University while Robert Penn Warren and Cleanth Brooks were teaching there and contributed some of his earliest stories to the *Southern Review*. Born in 1917, he can be considered among the first of the second or "middle generation" of Southern Renaissance writers.

Although Taylor's tales of seemingly conventional domestic life are quietly unfolded, just beneath the placid, almost unruffled surface of a world of families, businesses, servants, and life-as-usual on which the attention of the narrator seems to be focused there is always a possibility, and sometimes an almost assured certainty, of deep tragedy, disorder, and impending doom. This world of apparent order and matter-of-factness, which, as Robert Penn Warren says, Taylor "has made his own forever," is one that demonstrates graphically and compellingly a disintegrating tradition, the deterioration of the family, the loneliness of a life without aim or purpose.[9] Taylor presents a modern materialistic world of hurry, efficiency, and constant anxieties, the tendency of moderns to reduce concrete particularities to abstractions in order to avoid facing the sterility and hopelessness of their existence.

In "The Long Fourth," Harriet Wilson, a middle-aged wife of a well-to-do Nashville doctor, finally comes to realize that hers is a life without hope because she is incapable of either giving or receiving human affection. "Venus, Cupid, Folly, and Time" not only describes spiritual incest but suggests as well the possibility of physical incest in a supposedly respectable family. "Cookie" unmistakably presents the emptiness and the meaninglessness of the marriage of a middle-aged couple because the wife, caught in a loveless union, is unable to confront the devastating fact of her husband's infidelity. She has convinced herself that perhaps it isn't true, but if it is, the pain will be easier to bear if she does not admit the glaringly evident truth, even to herself. One of Taylor's best-known stories, "A Wife of Nashville," probes the tragic results of a father and mother's attempting to relegate their familial duties and pieties to domestic servants. Edmund

---

9. See Thomas Daniel Young, *Tennessee Writers* (Knoxville, 1981), 92ff.

Harper of "Guests" is forced to face the realities of his life by a visit from his wife's distant cousin. Cousin Johnny dies during the visit, and the shock of his death brings Edmund to confront the paucities of what he had believed to be a completely satisfying life. He addresses the dead Johnny:

> "You buried yourself alive on that farm of yours, I buried myself in my work here. But something in the life out there didn't satisfy you in the way it should. The country wasn't itself anymore. And something was wrong for me here. By 'country' we mean the old world, don't we . . .—the old ways, the old life, where people had real grandfathers and real children, and where love was something that could endure the light of day—something real. . . . Our trouble was, Cousin Johnny, we were lost without our old realities. . . . Other people seem to know some reason why it is better to be alive than dead this April morning. . . . There must be something."

Few other writers have expressed more forcefully the futility that one can feel in a world of uncurbed acquisitive materialism. Man is indeed like the blind crab in Allen Tate's poem: "He has energy but no purposeful world in which to use it."[10]

In *The Tennessee: The New River, Civil War to TVA* (1948), Donald Davidson criticized the manner in which the TVA obtained the land upon which the Tennessee River was to be converted into a chain of quiet lakes. Although the TVA officials realized that flooding the land to build the lakes would "retire from civilization large acres of fertile soil" that the farmers of the area were reluctant to give up, the directors and their staff of experts argued that the project would provide sufficient social and economic improvements to more than compensate the farmers for any inconvenience they might suffer. But the TVA officials, Davidson argued, using abstract thinking—the only kind of which they were capable—were unaware of the genuine human suffering their intrusion might effect:

> Because of its encroachments, there would be removals of many a family from homes where, in symbol or in fact, the Revolutionary sword or the pioneer rifle still hung above the mantel. Hearth fires would be extinguished that were as old as The Republic itself. Old landmarks would vanish; old graveyards would be obliterated; the

---

10. Taylor, *Collected Stories*, 437; Allen Tate, "Narcissus as Narcissus," in Tate, *Essays of Four Decades* (Chicago, 1968), 598.

ancient mounds of the Indian, which had resisted both the plow of the farmer and the pick of the curiosity seeker, would go under water. There would be tears, and gnashing of teeth, and lawsuits. There might even be feud and bloodshed."[11]

Davidson also feared the destruction of family unity that would result from razing so many homes: "The majority of the willing were the young folks. . . . The worst tragedy of the removal was in the fate of the older folks. They were genuinely reluctant to let the waters take the acres where they had spent their lives. They could not think of [separated families] . . . and living elsewhere. For many of these, death was hastened by the removal."[12]

In his novel *A Buried Land* (1963), Davidson's former student Madison Jones transforms the principles of Davidson's argument, to use one of Ransom's favorite terms, into the "common actuals." The prospects of flooding a small town in east Tennessee effect an irreconcilable difference between a young man and his father. The son, Percy Youngblood, argues that the lake is a progressive move to modernize the county. It will bring "electric power for all kinds of things," he says, "like pumps to bring water into people's houses." The father responds, "It'll bring water into their houses, all right." Percy tries to convince his father through what seems to him incontrovertible logic. The development of the dams, he continues, will help the poor people of the country by bringing industry. "Industry," the father says contemptuously; "you ever seen any industry? . . . Stink, and people swarming in from God knows where. . . . Living like a warren of rabbits and not thinking of a thing but their bellies." When his father asserts that his family already has a decent living, Percy responds that there are many families that don't, like the Bushnells. The father responds heatedly:

> "I was looking at the Bushnells before you was born. They are a no account lot, like the old man was before them. And they'll go right on being no account no matter what you try to do to Rhine County." His voice was still controlled but it had risen: and his eyes had begun the little fitful dance that came when his temper reached a point. But

---

11. Donald Davidson, *The Tennessee: The New River, Civil War to TVA* (New York, 1948), 237.
12. *Ibid.*, 257.

Percy seemed only the bolder: he was not now afraid to look straight back at his father. . . .

"It's *not* the same as stealing." And now he met his father straight on, eyes and voice. "Can't you see it's not? They can't let a few stand in the way of the rest. They'll pay you and pay you well, they always do. And find you a—"

"They can't pay me for this. And what kind of buying is it to point your gun and throw your money down?"[13]

If the "modern" reader were tempted to agree with Percy at first, his or her faith in "progress" must be shaken by this point.

Although both father and son try on several occasions to make up their differences, the bond is broken. The son leaves home and begins working for one of the crews building the dam. His mother, Rachel, worries that Percy never comes to visit the family, and she is particularly disappointed that he ignores her special invitation to join them on the date they are going to move their buried kin before the water covers their graves. Later, in town, Rachel sees her son and is appalled that he seems to regard her as a stranger. The truth comes to her with tragic conviction: The tie that held her family together has been severed, and the tradition of the Youngbloods on the land will cease with the death of her husband Tracy and the inundation of the homeplace.

While the action related above is occurring, Percy becomes involved in a very nasty situation, one that does much to reveal his true character. With the help of a ne'er-do-well about town, Percy seduces Cora Kincaid, whose brother Fowler is unnaturally protective of her because she is the only family he has. When Cora becomes pregnant, Percy and his friend, Jesse, take her to a Nashville abortionist who botches the operation, and Cora bleeds to death. In the dead of the night, Jesse and Percy bury her body in a place that is soon to be covered in a hundred feet of water. A frenzied Fowler goes in search of his sister, vowing to spend the rest of his life in the pursuit if necessary. He goes frantically to Nashville, becoming desperate when he realizes the impossibility of finding her among the most people he's ever seen in one place at one time in his life. Returning confused

---

13. Madison Jones, *A Buried Land* (New York, 1963), 26–27. Hereinafter cited by page number in the text.

and almost crazy, he walks toward the dam and accidentally comes within a few feet of where his sister is buried:

> Some broken cornstalks spiked the water or lay afloat on its surface. They would soon be under—very soon. . . . [He kept walking toward the dam until he] could see it clear, the dam outspread from flank to flank of the hills, as huge and shining white as if God's own hand had built it. As always when he saw it like this, he felt a kind of awe that instantly sank into a depression. He thought how the hands had not been God's at all, and how you could not trust any more in the strength of the things that His had made. (*BL*, 65)

Moments later, he kills one of the thoughtless dam workmen who speaks carelessly of Cora, and he is sent to prison for manslaughter.

The novel's conflict (the effect of flooding the land upon family unity) and its complication (the developments that make family reunion impossible) have been fully presented, and the action continues eight years later. Percy's brother Daryll has been killed in World War II, and a corpseless casket has been returned. This casket Rachel buries near the grave of Daryll's father, whose own death has surely been hastened by the loss of his land and grief for his lost son, Percy.

Although the Percy his father has loved is surely gone, he is not dead. Wounded and discharged from the army, he has completed law school. At the insistence of Rachel, he accompanies her to visit the graves of his father and brother. Rachel is obviously disappointed that Percy's return has made no difference in his feeling toward his family. "Ma," he says, "I'm sorry I couldn't get here when Pa died. The doctor said I oughtn't to. It's so far from California" (*BL*, 73). Waiting for him to continue, she realizes he has said all he intends, and that she has nothing to say to him.

In fact the concept of family among the Youngbloods has dissolved with the destruction of the home. Not only does Rachel feel out of place in her new house, but she can hardly make her way around in the strange town that has sprung up since the dam was built, on sidewalks filled with unfamiliar faces in front of stores she can never remember having seen before. Everything has changed so much that she can hardly find her way to Duke's Grocery, where, in one scene, she is supposed to meet her daughter, Liza. She is afraid to cross the streets—teeming with cars, delivery vans, and huge transport trucks—because she does not understand exactly how the traffic lights work and does not trust them. Her daughter, married and living with her husband and two children in a nearby town, has learned to cope with all the changes. Liza backs into the street with "astonishing confidence," moves the car "like a fish among all those headless machines that stopped and started and honked around her . . . ; that light flashing red and green and yellow did not make a ripple in her expression" (*BL*, 76).

As Rachel sits and looks at her daughter, though she can recognize her "pa's straight nose and sharp cheek bones and eyes goosegray," she realizes that she is almost as far removed from Liza as she is from Percy. She is as much alone, as Peter Taylor says of a character in one of his stories, "as if her children had died in childhood" (*BL*, 75–76).

Percy becomes a partner of Edgar Cadenhead, the most progressive and enterprising lawyer in the rapidly growing town, and Edgar directs his career carefully—assigning him the right cases and introducing him to the proper people—so that he will not only have a prosperous and satisfying law career but also the opportunity to enter politics if he wishes. An intelligent and ambitious young man, Percy seems well on his way to fulfilling Edgar's dream for him when specters from his past come back to plague him. First, he cannot rid himself of Jesse, who is always nearby to remind him of his complicity in the death of Cora Kincaid and to warn him that her brother Fowler is back in town, still trying to solve the mystery of his sister's death. Then he has an affair with Dorcas Baker, a maid at his boarding house, and only after he has revealed too much about a girl he once knew who died under conditions similar to those of Cora Kincaid does he discover that his mistress knows Fowler Kincaid. The most important result of his relationship with Dorcas, however, is that he comes to realize why he is always finding excuses not to marry the girl to whom he has been engaged for three years: He cannot experience human affection. "Love itself was an intangible: except when his blood was hot, how could any man among all the excitements and pressures of the world ever be sure in his mind that he had it? Maybe, in the sense he sought to probe, it was not anything; there was only blood to bring two people together and hold them in that posture until habit, disguising itself, stamped them with sufficient mutual needs and desires" (*BL,* 104).

Soon after he reaches this conclusion, he accepts a case, in spite of Edgar's objections, to defend Lonnie Washington, a youth who had killed his brutish father who was beating him. Apparently, Percy unconsciously sees some relationship between Lonnie and himself; at any rate, he can and does build a case of self-defense. As the case is nearing its end, and Percy has obviously been doing well, he suddenly becomes detached during a passionate cross-examination of Lonnie by the prosecutor. Seemingly unaware of what is going on, he leaves the courtroom before the case is concluded and disappears. Rachel later goes with him to the spot where their home had stood, now a dry, wasted lakebed. He almost incoherently admits his culpability in Cora's death, and implies his responsibility for Fowler's (whom he more-or-less accidentally hit with his car) and even for his father's demise. He vows to go back and accept his punishment. Rachel feels an odd sense of relief, though she knows that this act will be the end of the Youngbloods, who for so many generations had inhabited this valley. Jones's moving descriptions of the land, before and after its spoliation, are integrally linked with images of the old home and the family, now present only in Rachel's failing vision.

In an essay written in the spring of 1939, E. B. White makes us acutely aware of the deterioration of the quality of life in Concord, Massachusetts, and reminds us of the many similarities between Thoreau's requirements for the good life and those of the Agrarians. The essay takes the form of a letter to Thoreau. As White portrays himself driving into Concord, he observes a woman cutting grass with a motorized lawn mower. "What made me think of you [he informs Thoreau] is that the machine had gotten away from her . . . and in the brief glimpse I got of her it appeared to me that the lawn was mowing the lady." There is no question of what is riding whom here. This first encounter is premonitory of what will characterize the entire visit. The sounds he hears, as he stops before the inn, are different from those reported by Thoreau in *Walden:*

> In front of the Reuben Brown house a Buick was drawn up. At the wheel, motionless, his hat upon his head, a man sat, listening to Amos and Andy on the radio. . . . The deep voice of Andrew Brown, emerging from the car, although it originated more than two hundred miles away, was unstrained by distance. When you used to sit on the shore of your pond on Sunday morning, listening to the church bells of Acton and Concord, you were aware of the excellent filter of the intervening atmosphere. Science has attended to that, and sound maintains its intensity without regard for distance. Properly sponsored, it goes on forever.

He informs Thoreau, too, that "your fellow-townsmen were stirring abroad," not many walking, but most of them in their cars; "and the sound which they made in Concord at evening was a rustling and a whispering. . . . Automobiles, skirting a village green, are like flies that have gained the inner ear—they buzz, pause, start, stop, halt, break, and the whole effect is a nervous polytone curiously disturbing."[14]

Walking from the village to Thoreau's hallowed pond the following morning, he is immediately aware that he is approaching his destination:

> I knew I must be nearing your woodland retreat when the Golden Pheasant Lunchroom came into view—Sealtest ice cream, toasted sandwiches, hot frankfurters, waffles, tonics, and lunches. Were I the proprietor, I should add rice, Indian meal, and molasses—just for old time's sake. The Pheasant, incidentally, is for sale: a chance for some nature lover who wishes to set himself up beside a pond in the Concord atmosphere and live deliberately, fronting only the essential facts of life on Number 126. Beyond the Pheasant was a place called Walden Breezes. . . . Behind the Breezes, in a sun-parched clearing, dwelt your philosopher descendents in their trailers, each trailer the size of your hut, but all grouped together for the sake of congeniality.[15]

Thoreau's attempt to simplify his life, to try to find out how much of the world's goods, how much company and how much solitude he needed to live life to its fullest, has become a mere farce. The woman with the mowing machine is clear evidence that

---

14. E. B. White, *One Man's Meat* (New York, 1980), 80, 83–84.
15. *Ibid.*, 84–85.

"things are in the saddle and ride mankind." The unnecessarily complicated life of modern man, with its promises of life without work or worry, has become a confused, crowded, but essentially empty dream. As Thoreau and the Agrarians had both insisted, man must control his life, give it aim and purpose, if his earthly existence is to be complete and satisfying.

Many modern southern novelists, apparently, have reached the same conclusion. Stephen Goodwin's *The Blood of Paradise* (1979), for example, traces the attempts of Estes Herschel Steadman, his wife, Anna, and their daughter, Maggie, to escape from an increasingly demanding materialistic society. Goodwin, born in 1943, is one of the new generation of southern writers, with no direct ties to the first-generation Agrarians. He grew up in Brewton, Alabama, and took his B.A. from Harvard and his M.A. from the University of Virginia, where he studied creative writing with Peter Taylor. Although he has taught at several colleges and universities in the Washington area and is now on the faculty of George Mason University, most of his writing is done on his farm in Williamsville, Virginia.

In *The Blood of Paradise,* Goodwin styles his hero as the son of a successful accountant and the grandson of an even more successful land speculator, whom he idolizes. Steadman, as he prefers to be called, is destined for a life in high finance. He dutifully attends college, expecting to concentrate on business administration and economics, but his plans are frustrated when he becomes the prodigy of a sadistic and alcoholic creative writing teacher, and between alcoholic binges and sexual orgies he finds time to begin a novel but is unable to complete it. He finishes college, nevertheless, and goes to Washington to become an assistant to Congressman Bunny Biggs, a position his grandfather has secured for him. While there, he meets Anna and marries her when she is three months pregnant with his child. Soon he becomes disenchanted with his job, takes the proceeds from a trust fund provided by his grandfather, and goes for a six-month sojourn in Europe, where Anna, who had studied art, looks at paintings and Steadman spends his time trying to complete his novel and writing two stories. Although he sells the stories, both publishers to whom he sends his novel return it. He enrolls in law school, which he later decides was "a blunder, worse than a blunder, a failure of nerve."[16] Out of frustration, he begins to rewrite his novel. Even this activity, however, cannot relieve the boredom of law school or the tensions of a disintegrating marriage, so he begins to think more and more about purchasing a place he knows of in southwestern Virginia, an old rundown farm with a house about to fall in, surrounded by a cluster of decaying outbuildings. He uses most of his trust fund to purchase the place, and he and his wife and daughter move in.

Most of the winter is consumed in mopping, scrubbing, painting, and mending, trying to make the place habitable. The Steadmans do most of the work themselves, with occasional assistance from friendly neighbors and the members of a nearby commune-like community (ironically called Xanaduc). Even with the coming of spring, Steadman and Anna are so fully occupied with the house that they hardly notice the beauties that crowd around them, though they both are aware that their personal relations are much improved. As time permits, Steadman writes on his novel or takes long walks through the mountainous country that surrounds their place. For the first time, Anna becomes aware of birds and flowers: "A pair of bluebirds nested in a hollow locust near the garden. Goldfinches sunned themselves on the power line. The evening grosbeaks always in a gang, always in a noisy flutter, making dashing swirls around the trees, giftwrapping them. . . . And flowers: during those mongrel days of March and April when the great display came forth, she tried to draw them" (*BP*, 73). For the first time she sees, really sees, the particular, concrete objects she is trying to recreate, and she tries for "stark, literal accuracy. Every serration on every leaf, every vein and fluting, every division and dint of blossom" (*BP*, 73–74). She becomes convinced, as she studies these objects, that she has some talent for the art she has half-heartedly been trying to practice for a good many years.

As the place gradually begins to take shape—the kitchen modernized with new appliances, floor covering, and fresh paint; a new indoor bathroom, with all the conveniences installed—Anna thinks she has never seen Steadman happier. He looks like

---

16. Stephen Goodwin, *The Blood of Paradise* (New York, 1979), 38. Hereinafter cited by page number in the text.

a man who has really found a place for himself in the world; he is "someone from somewhere." She knows, finally, that she really cares for him and he for her. They both adore little Maggie, spending hours talking to her or watching her play the games that amuse her:

> One May morning Steadman was finishing up the cabinets in the kitchen. Through the open window he could see Anna and Maggie out in the garden, their companionable murmur. He glanced at them now and then in the rich black plot—Anna, who'd never owned a houseplant, was out of bed early now to run down to her garden to see what had happened overnight. She still didn't quite believe that all those seeds did what they were supposed to do. Before planting she'd made a map of her garden, marking off the territory of each vegetable; now, when she marked on it the dates of planting and germination, she regarded it, Steadman thought, with some wonder, as if the documents were responsible for what was happening in the garden. This morning she and Maggie had the string and stakes, planting beans. (*BP*, 86)

They are happy, as he is, and he finds in his contentment that he is more pleased with his writing than he has ever been.

But things begin to go awry in Eden, and here, I think, is where Goodwin's novel becomes untracked. First, Anna's mother telephones that Kay, Anna's twin sister, is taking drugs again and associating with a "bad crowd." Although Anna is half tempted to answer her mother's plea for help and go to Washington, she doesn't want to leave Steadman and Maggie. The last thing she expects to happen does: Kay shows up at the farm, much emaciated and nervous. A child of the sixties, she has no inhibitions and lies around, sometimes naked, in the sun. Anna is alarmed that she looks so pathetic, alone, and hopeless, and she tries unsuccessfully to regain some of the closeness the sisters had once had. It is obvious that Kay is intended to demonstrate the kind of person Anna would have become if she had remained in the city. All Anna accomplishes is to distance herself from Steadman, who grows grumpy and fractious. Anna begins to discover snakes, bugs, and a mad fox among the birds and flowers.

Kay goes to a party at the commune, has too many drugs, and goes berserk, after Anna, fearing what might happen, has already gone home. Steadman stays until the party is over, becomes interested in a girl named Peggy, goes home frustrated, and calls Anna a coward because she had refused to stay and help cope with Kay. In her turmoil Anna discovers she is pregnant and, despite her love for Maggie, decides to have an abortion to spite Steadman, who would not only forgive her but also "would have worshipped her, his vessel." On this flimsy bit of rationalization, she goes back to Washington on the pretext of seeing her family and has an abortion of which Steadman is unaware. Here, as in Jones, abortion is a key symbol of deteriorating family values. Since Anna has apparently followed Kay to Washington, Steadman believes that Anna's attachment to Kay is sronger than her love for him, and he has an affair with Peggy. Their coupling is merely the result of physical passion, an ephemeral episode that has nothing to do with his love for Anna and is not particularly satisfying to him. However, while Anna is recuperating from the abortion, Kay is killed in an automobile accident (a possible suicide). The end of the novel is somewhat ambiguous, but the reader is expected to believe, apparently, that Anna will return to Steadman and the two will resume their lives together, reconciled.

This ending is not convincing because the book has changed its system of morals at about its center. In the first half of the book, living on the farm in accord with the natural cycle of life is as wholesome as life was on the farm described by Lytle in "The Hind Tit," but somewhere this rather simplistic system of knowing good and bad is altered to include the permissive morality of the 1960s. The fact that Anna and Steadman found happiness under the first system, approved by the Agrarians and the transcendentalists, makes the second seem unlikely, even incompatible. Ransom had insisted in "Forms and Citizens" that only human beings in a society that allows them to practice the "aesthetic forms" are capable of knowing the complex human emotion that Milton, Spenser, Sidney, and others have described as human love. Like all other animals, the human being feels lust, but this basically uncomplicated passion is elevated to love only through a series of carefully regulated social conventions beginning, for Ransom, with the coming-out party and going through the rituals of dating, engagement, and marriage. This social order is the means by which man controls his primitive urges and becomes civilized. What he feels in the beginning for *all* members of the opposite sex, he comes to feel for only *one*.¹⁷ Ransom would argue, therefore, that the Steadman of the end of the book has shown no more aptitude for human love than Kay has, and this lack would likely destroy him as it did her. The Transcendentalist would perceive that Steadman's feelings for Peggy did not come from the *me*, the part of man that he shares with the Over-Soul (or God), but from the *not-me*, his connection with the lower animals. Goodwin's style—abrupt, graphic, accommodating four-letter words with ease—also seems at odds with his willingness to let his characters live happily ever after.

A member of Madison Jones's generation, West Virginian William Hoffman has written since the early fifties eight novels and a collection of short stories that consider the human condition in twentieth-century America. A graduate of Hampden-Sydney College in Virginia and a sometime teacher there, Hoffman also studied at the Iowa Writers' Workshop. In *The Land That Drank the Rain* (1982), Hoffman takes a slightly different approach to what one must possess to be truly human. Outwardly, he comes nearer to advocating the specific approach of Thoreau than that of any of the Nashville Agrarians. At the conclusion of *Walden,* Thoreau tells precisely why he went to live there: "I went to the woods because I wished to live deliberately, to front only the essential facts of life, to see if I could not learn what it had to teach. . . . I wanted to live deep and suck out the marrow of life, . . . to drive life into a corner and reduce it to its lowest possible terms."¹⁸

Claytor Carson, the protagonist of Hoffman's novel, wants to simplify his life. A salesman, builder, and successful land developer in California, he has almost everything offered by a twentieth-century materialistic society—wealth, a spacious home, closets full of sharkskin suits, and obsessive, perverse sex. His life is infinitely more complicated than Thoreau's was; therefore he has more trouble reducing it to its barest essentials. First he has to make two trips from California to the Cumberland Mountains of Kentucky to find the place where he wants to settle; Thoreau had merely to walk outside the village where he lived to find Walden Pond. Thoreau "squatted" on the land with the per-

17. For a fuller discussion of this topic, see Thomas Daniel Young, *The Past in the Present: A Thematic Study of Modern Southern Fiction* (Baton Rouge, 1981), 14–30.
18. Thoreau, *Walden*, 64.

mission of a friend; Carson has to pay the owner of the apparently worthless piece of mountainside $28,500 for his opportunity to "live deep and suck out the marrow of life." His basic needs, to be sure, are considerably more than Thoreau's, who with the help of some friends and a borrowed ax built his house, planted his garden, and lived for six months for $61.99 3/4. In a catalog that burlesques Thoreau, Carson takes

> a sleeping bag, an ax, a hatchet, a sheath knife, a flashlight, friction tape, a spiral notebook, a broom, an iron skillet, cutlery, pots, pans, two galvanized buckets, a plastic bucket, a Remington automatic shotgun, shells, tin plates and cups, an ice chest, a hoe, an iron rake, a pick, a sledge, steel wedges, a handsaw, a bucksaw, a hammer, nails, a chisel, a T square, a plane, a trowel, a level, a file, a tape measure, a whetstone, a lantern, two kerosene lamps, a sewing kit, a yellow slicker, a sou'wester, a county map, binoculars, a woodburning stove, soap, tooth paste, condiments, coffee, canned goods, twine, a nylon rope, clothes, shoes, boots, thermal longjohns, a washtub, two shovels, a grubbing hoe, barn matches, a first-aid kit, packets of seed wrapped in polyethylene, and also wrapped in polyethylene $20,000, all $50 bills, each new and unsullied.[19]

The packets of money he carefully buries in several different hiding places.

A few comments would seem in order as we think of this list of Carson's minimal needs—as he conceived of them—as compared with Thoreau's: First of all, Carson's tastes were more cultivated and more sophisticated than Thoreau's; then, it would seem, Carson attempted to anticipate his every need, whereas Thoreau merely indicated what he immediately required and later itemized the food, clothes, and seed he would eventually want. It has been said, of course, that Thoreau "was never beyond the sound of Emerson's dinner bell," that he deliberately stayed near and in touch with friends and neighbors. We know he entertained at Walden, visited and attended meetings in the village, went huckleberry picking with friends, and did day labor to help earn his keep. Carson, however, thinks the world so profane he wants to cut every possible tie with it.

On his first night in Kentucky, Carson burns the yellow Cadillac he has driven from California (with 16,073.9 miles on the odometer), his credit cards, his country club memberships, and

19. William Hoffman, *The Land That Drank the Rain* (Baton Rouge, 1982), 3.

his watch, and goes to sleep in the best of the three dilapidated shacks on his property. The next morning he looks around for the best place for his garden and a building site for his house. One is reminded of how fully Thoreau was engaged in these last two activities for many months so that he could determine the minimum essentials of the productive life, but Carson is trying to make his break from an acquisitive materialistic society immediate and complete. He refuses his mail (like Thoreau he has "no need for the post office"), and when he has to go into town he tries to keep communication to the absolute minimum by feigning dumbness and lameness. Carson has much more difficulty avoiding the "life of quiet desperation" than Thoreau did, because the officials of the county demand that he receive his mail, respond to it, and do the other "duties of a useful citizen." Despite these impediments, Carson isolates himself and tries to live frugally, independently, and "as deliberately as Nature." He plants a garden (30' by 50'), makes a place in the stream so that he can have adequate and sanitary drinking water, and builds himself a more comfortable cabin. Like Thoreau, he builds his own furniture, making sure that it fits his precise needs. Unlike Thoreau's, Carson's labors are always being interrupted by some official telling him what his duties to society are and what civilization demands. Nevertheless, he avoids every contact with the outside world he can and feels cleaner than he has since he was a child. So devoted is he to his new solitude that he can easily fend off his former business partner, who comes offering him the opportunity to earn a million dollars, and his wife, Bea, who tries to entice him with the perverse sexual adventures he had once found so captivating, not because she wants him back but because she wants his assistance in a business deal.

After two years, two months, and two days at Walden, Thoreau had learned what he wanted to know and returned peacefully to civilization. Carson is not so fortunate; however, he finds the demands of society harder to ignore. Just as he has completed the physical means of enjoying individual freedom, he experiences a personal involvement that requires him to negate everything he has attempted. An unexpected event engages his full participation: Vestil Shank, a wild and unloved boy who, we are told, "could have been fathered by any member of a football squad in the back of a school bus coming from a game," is recruited by the town madam as a male prostitute, and Carson's courageous and self-sacrificing human feelings assert themselves. It is no coincidence that Carson's new troubles begin, as his old ones did, with sex and money. He surrenders his hard-earned self-sufficiency so that Vestil can escape the town and live. Giving Vestil the last of his money under the guise of paying him a "professional" visit, Carson fights and suffers facial mutilation to spring Vestil free and get him on a bus out of town. Like Thoreau, when he reduced life to its barest essentials, Carson found it good. More importantly, as the Agrarians before him, he believed that one does not have to surrender his soul to an unrestrained, acquisitive materialistic society. The dark, grotesque humor that masks serious contemplation of moral issues in Hoffman's novel takes him a long way from Thoreau in the texture of his fiction, though he remains close to Thoreau in spirit.

Thoreau said that he left Walden because he had many more lives to live and could not spare any further time for that one. Undoubtedly, he thought he had learned from his experience all he could. What he had suspected, he found was true: that the needless clutter of urban centers tends to corrupt man and places unnecessary obstacles in his way as he attempts to live the good life. What Thoreau's life at Walden demonstrates, above all else, is that human life can be lived in tune with the natural cycle, the seasonal change from summer to autumn, winter, and spring. When he left the woods amid the burgeoning of spring, he was conscious of new life within him, a spiritual rebirth, so that he was able to proclaim the goodness of life properly lived. The impression modern writers of fiction get from *I'll Take My Stand* is not far different from the message Thoreau was going to "brag" about "as lustily as chanticleer in the morning." They see the Agrarians as rightly protesting the amount of wasted effort in a technocratic society and join them in bemoaning the concerted attacks on man's basic humanity.

It is unfortunate that the symposium of the Nashville group has the word *agrarian* in its subtitle, because to many readers it means either subsistence farming or utopian conservatism, impeding progress and turning the clock backwards to a time that never existed except in the imagination of a few antebellum idealists. It is a good thing that most of the Agrarians were not advocating a wholesale return to the soil, because we know that in the past fifty years farming has become as commercialized and as dependent on high finance as any enterprise in which man is engaged. We read in the agricultural journals of farms operated by one man from a bubble-top control tower through the use of computers, radio, radar, and—possibly—atomic power. On these farms, people have learned, through irrigation and temperature-control, the means of conquering their most unpredictable adversary: nature. This is not the kind of farm visualized by Lytle or John Donald Wade; it is a frightening—because totally impersonal—view of what can happen when a society decides "to invest its resources in the applied sciences." Although the Agrarians could not have imagined a contemporary farm, they could have perceived the effect of such an institution on the human being. In the words of another Southern writer of the younger generation:

> [People] will not live where they work or work where they live. They will not work where they play. And they will not, above all, play where they work. There will be no singing in those fields. There will be no crews of workers of neighbors laughing and joking, telling stories, or competing at tests of speed or strength or skill. There will be no holiday walks or picnics in those fields because, in the first place, the fields will be ugly, all graces of nature having been ruled out, and, in the second place, they will be dangerous.[20]

The significance of *I'll Take My Stand* to the contemporary novelist, then, is its cry of outrage at the attempts of man to deify the machine and its prime mover, money. It is a passionate cry against the attempt to create a materialist society in which only the "economic forms" are respected. It is a firm pronouncement that no amount of social planning or scientific achievement will effect a perfect world inhabited by perfect individuals. It reiterates that the society that ignores the "aesthetic values" and the human spirit does so only at its own peril. Now, at a time when the destruction of all human life appears to be a possibility, if not a pleasant expectation, the philosophical musings of Thoreau and the Agrarians are perhaps more provocative and compelling than they have ever been.

(1985)

20. Wendell Berry, *The Untaming of America* (San Francisco, 1973), 74.

Index

Barrett, William, 95
Berryman, John, 100–101
Brooks, Cleanth, 1, 15, 48, 50–72, 101, 105
Bush, Douglas, 96–97

Chalmers, Gordon K., 90–91, 100, 102–103
Chalmers, Roberta T. (Schwartz), 90–91
Chew, Samuel C., 20, 22, 34
Coffin, Charles, 99–100, 103
Collins, Seward, 105–106
Cousins, Norman, 98
Cowley, Malcolm, 106

Davidson, Donald, 72, 76–77, 88–89, 107–41, 154, 156–57, 159–60
Davis, Robert Gorman, 104
Dos Passos, John, 101

Eliot, T. S., 24, 30, 35, 37, 62, 74, 86, 88, 92, 97
Empson, William, 37, 53
Evans, Luther H., 98

Faulkner, William, 1–18
Fletcher, John Gould, 98
Flint, John Cudworth, 77
Frost, Robert, 84–93
Fugitives, 22, 50–51

Goodwin, Stephen, 166–70
Gordon, Caroline, 126, 136–37

Hillyer, Robert, 95–106 *passim*
Hoffman, William, 170–73

I'll Take My Stand, 104–106, 153–57, 173–75

Jarrell, Randall, 76
Jones, Madison, 160–64
Justus, James H., 144–45, 152

Lobdell, D. H., 99–100
Lumpkins, Grace, 105–106
Lytle, Andrew, 154, 156–57, 169, 174

MacCaffrey, Isabel G., 83
MacLeish, Archibald, 100
Magner, James E., 71
Morley, Christopher, 84–85
Morris, Charles W., 36, 38–39

Odum, Howard W., 155–56

Pound, Ezra, 94–106 *passim*
Pratt, William C., 154–55

Ransom, John Crowe, 154, 156
—writings: "The Concrete Universal" (I, II, and III), 32–33, 43–49, 67; "Criticism, Inc.," 19–20, 57, 61; *God Without Thunder*, 35, 51; "Mixed Modes," 22–23, 34; *The New Criticism*, 30–31, 37–40; "Necrological," 80–83; "Old Age of an Eagle," 32, 42–43; "Poetry: A Note

in Ontology," 28–30, 35–36, 60–61; "Poetry: The Formal Analysis," 32, 65–66; "Prose: A Doctrine of Relativity," 24, 24–25; "Shakespeare at Sonnets," 52, 70, 73; "The Third Moment," 25–27, 35, 40, 69–70; "Thoughts on the Poetic Discontent," 23, 29, 34–35; "Wanted: An Ontological Critic," 21–22, 31, 36, 63; "Why Critics Don't Go Mad," 67–68; *The World's Body*, 22–23, 27, 34–35
Rice, Philip Blair, 99–100, 101, 103
Richards, I. A., 36–37
Robbins, Rossell Hope, 99
Rubin, Louis D., 154

Schoenberg, Ellen, 14
Shapiro, Karl, 94–96

Stevens, Wallace, 86, 92, 100
Strandberg, Victor, 146–47, 151–52
Sutcliffe, Denham, 99–100, 101–103

Tate, Allen, 24–28 *passim*, 32, 34–35, 36, 40, 52, 73, 76–77, 88, 95, 97, 100–101, 105–106, 109–10, 126–41 *passim*, 154, 159
Taylor, Peter, 157–59

Vickery, Olga, 14

Wade, John Donald, 174
Warren, Austin, 105
Warren, Robert Penn, 75, 78, 142–52, 154
White, E. B., 164–66
Wimsatt, W. K., 43
Winters, Yvor, 37, 104

WAKE TECHNICAL COMMUNITY COLLEGE LIBRARY
9101 FAYETTEVILLE ROAD
RALEIGH, NORTH CAROLINA 27603

3 3063 00061 1995

DATE DUE

MAY 2 1 1996			
MAR 2 ~~5~~ 1998			
APR 1 3 1998			
GAYLORD			PRINTED IN U.S.A.